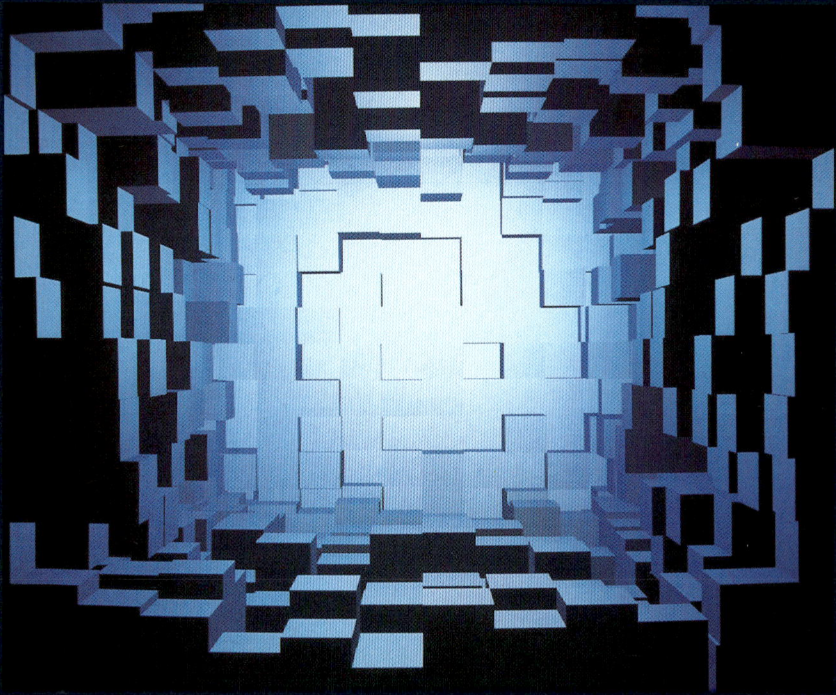

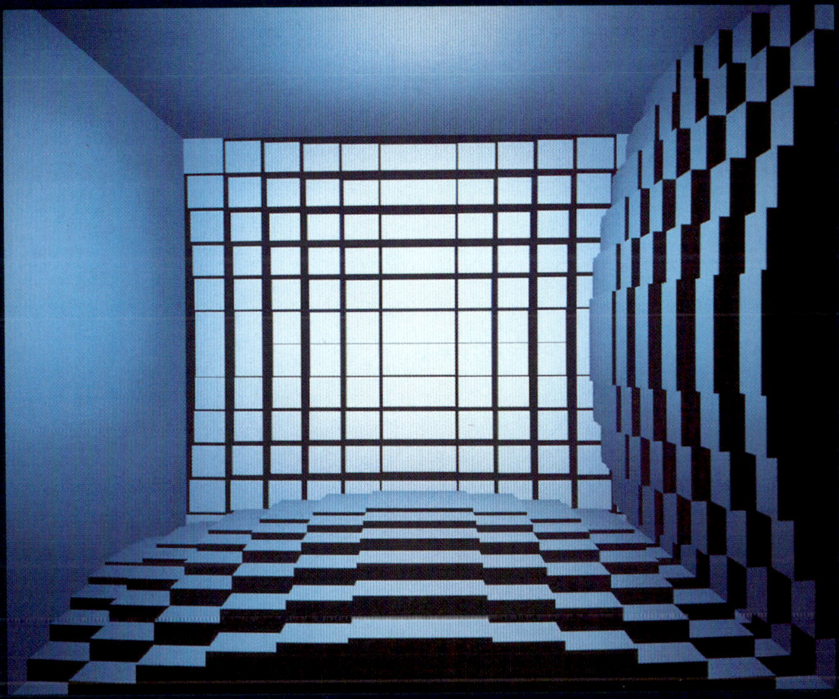

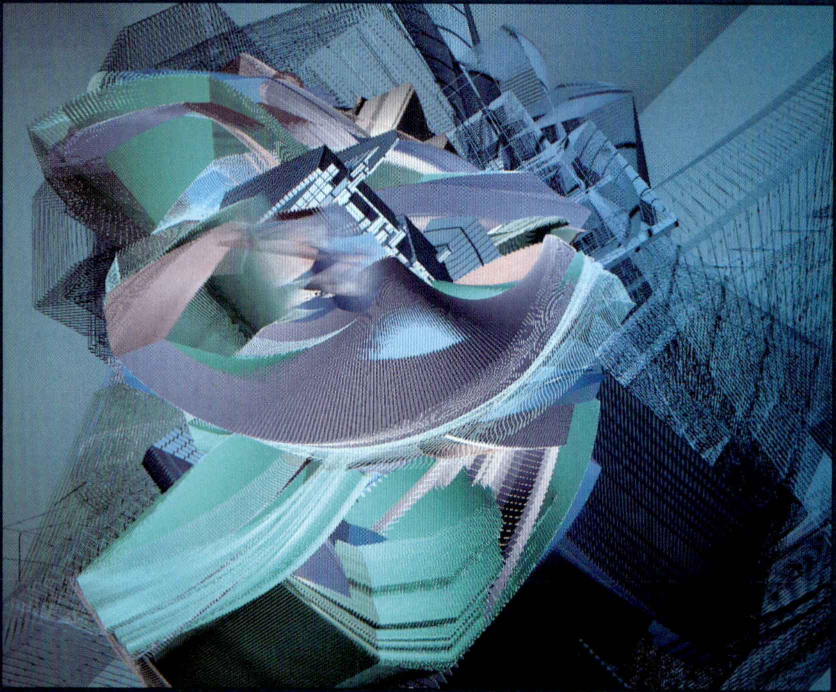

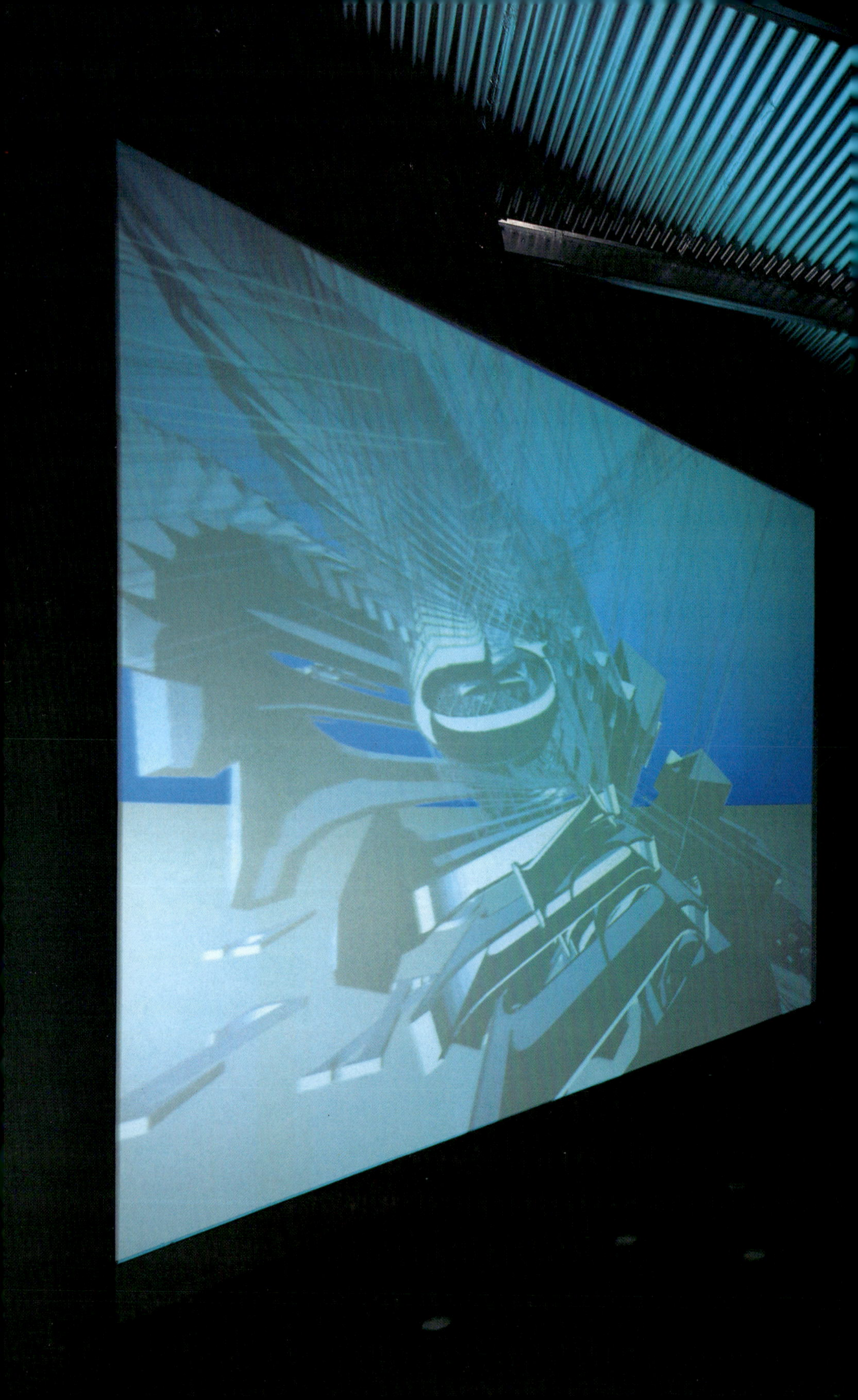

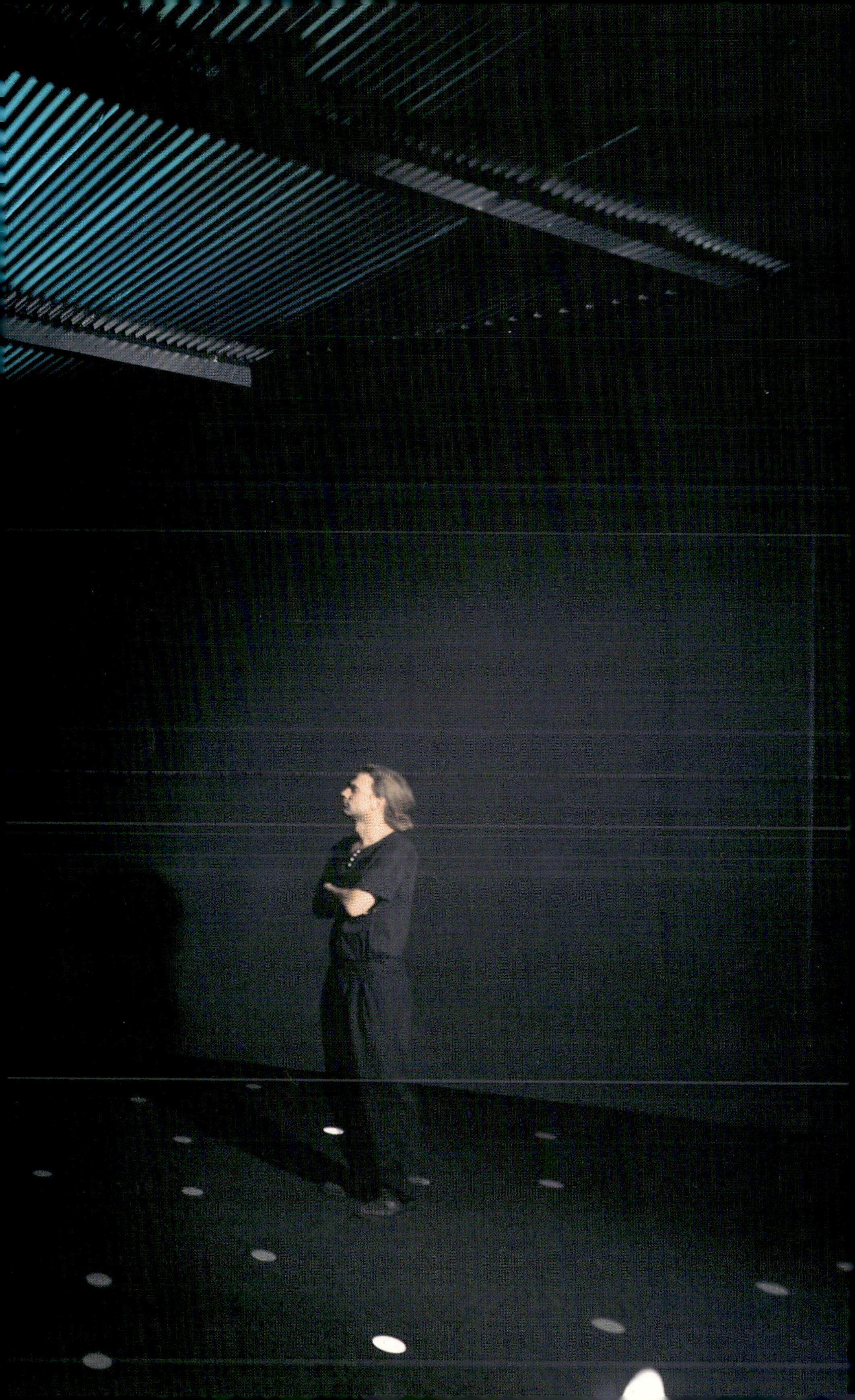

PETER WEIBEL

ZUR RECHTFERTIGUNG DER HYPOTHETISCHEN NATUR DER KUNST UND DER NICHT-IDENTITÄT IN DER OBJEKTWELT

ON JUSTIFYING THE HYPOTHETICAL NATURE OF ART AND THE NON-IDENTICALITY WITHIN THE OBJECT WORLD

Inhalt:

Susanne Craemer
Zur Rechtfertigung der hypothetischen Natur der Kunst und der Nicht-Identität in der Objektwelt

Eine interaktive Computerinstallation von Peter Weibel in der Galerie Tanja Grunert, Köln, 5. Juni – 1. August 1992

1. Die Installation

Den Besucher erwartet ein spitzwinkliger Raum, der über eine Stahlträgerkonstruktion aus Aluminiumblechplatten völlig abgedunkelt ist. Einzige Lichtquelle ist die 5 x 3,75 m große Leinwand. Sie ist die durchlässige (transparente) Seite des realen Environments, die die anderen, virtuellen Welten präsentieren wird. Den Grundriß des Environments (Architekt: Christian Möller) liefert das ‹Haus vom Nikolaus›, d. h. die Ansicht des in hiesigen Breitengraden gewöhnlichen Hauses mit Satteldach. An der linken ‹Dachseite› ist die Leinwand plaziert, die ein CAD-Datengroßbildprojektor bestrahlt (Rückprojektion). Mit seinem Eintritt in den abgedunkelten Raum eröffnet der Besucher nun das Spiel. Sobald er den mit grauen und farbigen Punkten perforierten Boden betreten hat, muß er sich entscheiden: entweder bleibt er – sofern er die farbigen Punkte meidet – auf dem Boden der Realität, oder er springt von dem realen

Environment in ein virtuelles, indem er auf einen roten, grünen oder blauen Bodenpunkt tritt. Mit diesem Schritt wählt er eine von mehreren möglichen virtuellen Welten aus, indem er auf die übrigen, hellgrauen Punkte des ausgelegten Teppichs tritt, navigiert er durch die einmal ausgewählte virtuelle Welt und deren Ereignishorizont. Der Besucher kann also zwischen virtueller und realer sowie zwischen drei virtuellen Welten hin und her springen. Hat er einen Weltmodus betreten, steuert er mit seinem weiteren Spaziergang über die hellgrauen Bodenpunkte die Erscheinungsweise, die Formen und Gestalten der jeweiligen Welt. Er wählt somit nicht nur die Codes der verschiedenen ‹Weltweisen› (world modes), sondern spielt, weitergehend, mit den Modulen dieser Codes. Seine Schritte evozieren wechselnde Bilder dieser Welten, die in Echtzeit auf der riesigen Leinwand erscheinen.

Was ist, vor seinen konkreten Bildern, die Voraussetzung dieses in Echtzeit vermittelten sprunghaften Spaziergangs in virtuellen Welten? Zunächst ist der Boden, das aktive Areal der Installation, mit einer Anzahl von Sensoren unterlegt, die auf der Oberfläche markiert sind: das Betreten des roten, grünen oder blauen Punkts aktiviert eine der drei virtuellen Welten, das Betreten der hellgrauen, über den Raum verteilten 29 übrigen Punkte aktiviert anschließend die Formen und Gestalten der jeweiligen Welt auf der Leinwand. Der technische Hergang verläuft dabei wie folgt: Die Sensoren (Kontaktmatten) geben die An- oder Abwesenheit des Betrachters an ein von Bob O'Kane konstruiertes Circuit board weiter, das die 32 Schalter einer button box steuert, die den 32 Kontaktmatten zugeordnet sind. Diese Information löst dann in dem angeschlossenen Computer (Silicon Graphics 4D/320 VGX) numerische Operationen und Algorithmen nach den Programmen aus, die durch das anfängliche Aktivieren der farbig markierten Sensoren gewählt wurden. Die digital codierte Information wird nun in eine grafische (visuelle) Information umgewandelt und an einen Datenprojektor weitergeleitet, der als Video-Rückprojektion Bilder in Echtzeit auf die große Leinwand projiziert. Gideon May hat die Programme der verschiedenen virtuellen Welten so koordiniert, daß sie, über die realen Bodenpunkte aktiviert, im gemeinsamen virtuellen Raum auf der Leinwand nacheinander erscheinen können. Die Installation präsentiert sich somit in drei Teilen:

1. der Boden der Realität, der durch drei farbige und 29 hellgraue Punkte perforiert ist und den spazierenden Besucher zum Sprung in die virtuellen Welten auffordert;
2. die Verbindung dieser Interfaces mit den Programmen, die die verschiedenen Welten definieren;
3. die Bilder der Video-Rückprojektion auf einer Leinwand, die auf den Besucher unmittelbar in Echtzeit reagieren.

Über die Schnittstellen des Bodens reagiert die Installation direkt und interaktiv auf den Benutzer. Doch in Umkehrung seiner Situation vor der alphabetischen Tastatur etwa einer Schreibmaschine, ist er nicht in der Lage, die 32 Bodenpunkte instrumentell zu bedienen. Er selbst wird vielmehr von der nach dem Alphabet konstruierten Tastatur der Bodenkontakte ertastet. Der Betrachter wird von den Sensoren dieser riesigen Schreibmaschine wahrgenommen, vom Computer interpretiert und auf der Leinwand ausgedrückt. Der Betrachter wird selbst zum Werkzeug. Dieses System, das die instrumentelle Funktion üblicher Schreibsysteme pervertiert, bildet dennoch mit den 32 Bodentasten (3 world modes, 26 Buchstaben, 3 Sonderzeichen) ein Interface, das wie eine Sprache organisiert ist: sofern es nicht die Botschaft, sondern die Präsenz des Subjekts vermittelt und damit Wirklichkeit nicht wieder-, sondern die Bedingung ihrer Konstruktion vorgibt.

Die drei virtuellen Welten, die der Besucher per Rot-, Grün- oder Blaupunkt aktiviert, machen die verzerrende Wahrnehmung von Wirklichkeit nun in ungewohnter Weise augenfällig und erlebbar. Text-Welt, Raum-Welt und Objekt-Welt sind die drei zugänglichen virtuellen Welten. Zwischen ihnen kann der Betrachter hin und her springen. Durch die Aktivierung eines der farbigen Sensoren, wobei Grün der Textwelt, Rot der Objektwelt und Blau der Raumwelt zugeordnet sind, wird in eine der 3 möglichen virtuellen Welten eingetreten. Die folgenden 29 hellgrauen Sensoren aktivieren dann nur Veränderungen in der einmal gewählten Welt, solange keine andere Farbtastatur betreten wird. Mit dem Betreten eines anderen Farbpunktes erscheint eine andere virtuelle Welt. Wollte man die in fortschreitender Entstellung und Bewegung begriffenen drei Welten knapp beschreiben, vor der Interaktion mit dem Betrachter, so würde man folgende Aufnahme machen:

– ein leerer Innenraum (Raum-Welt)
– Buchstaben, Wörter bzw. Sätze (Text-Welt)
– Tisch, Stuhl, Gesicht (Objekt-Welt)

Ein Innenraum, mit Subjekt, Tisch und Stuhl, in dem Worte gewechselt werden, ist eine Aufnahme alltäglichster Erfahrung. Die drei Welt-Weisen brechen die Trivialität dieser alltäglichen Erfahrung nun radikal auf: die gewohnte Wirklichkeit von Innenraum, von Tisch, Stuhl, Gesicht und von sinnvollen Wörtern bzw. von Sätzen erscheint – wenn überhaupt – in diesen Welten als überhängiges Bild. Die Welt der konstanten Erscheinungen wird zu einer Welt der Variablen. Dadurch werden vertraute Vorstellungen von Identität und Wirklichkeit, von Subjekt- und Objekttrennungen in Frage gestellt. Nicht-Identität und Inkommensurabilität werden axiomatisch. Raum, Objekte und Text werden in diesen Welten bis zur Unkenntlichkeit durch den Beobachter bewegt und verformt, und zwar nach folgenden Parametern: Veränderlich und vom Betrachter bewegt ist in diesen Welten die Position der Elemente entlang der X, Y, Z-Achsen, ihre Skalierung, Proportion und ihre Rotation. Darüber hinaus steuert der Betrachter auch Sonderfunktionen: Twirl-, Twist-, Wave-Funktion etc., die Textur ändert sich zwischen den Objekten (von realer Textur zu Ziffern, Buchstaben etc. als Textur), zwischen den Objekten und der Wand wandert die Textur, wie in einem thermodynamischen System bleibt die Energie konstant, sodaß die Bewegung von einem Objekt zum anderen springt, statt Texturen gibt es gelegentlich Drahtmodelle, Bewegungsspuren bleiben durch eine Nicht-Lösch-Taste (Overdraw-Funktion), die Aggregatzustände der Phänomene ändern sich: opake Körper oder Drahtmodelle, Punkte oder Linien etc.

Raum, Text und Objekte ‹können› dementsprechend ‹Dinge› und folgen Gesetzen, die der alltäglichen Erfahrung definitiv widersprechen. Dabei machen sie in ihren jeweiligen Vermögen gegenseitige Anleihen. Worte werden gegenständlich und räumlich, Objekte mit einer Buchstaben-Textur überzogen und der Raum zerfällt in sich selbst gleiche Objekte. Mit diesem wechselseitigen Bezug und der nach nur wenigen Parametern erfolgenden Entstellung ihrer gewohnten Gestalt, präzisieren die virtuellen Welten ihre Erschütterung alltäglicher Wirklichkeitserfahrung.

2. Die Text-Welt

Der Spaziergänger hat nun einen farbigen Punkt betreten und ist in die virtuelle Welt der Sprache gesprungen. Die nach Entwürfen von Peter Weibel und von Constanze Ruhm designte Text-Welt (Programmierung: Bob O'Kane) präsentiert auf der Leinwand einen virtuellen Raum, auf dessen Boden sich die Buchstaben des Alphabets, angeordnet wie ein Keybord, befinden. Nun geht der Betrachter im realen Environment weiter bzw. ein anderer Betrachter tritt auf einen der 26 hellgrauen Kontaktpunkte, die den 26 Buchstaben des Alphabets zugeordnet sind.

Wird ein Buchstabe im virtuellen Raum aktiviert, löst sich nun dieser, sein Double zurücklassend, vom Boden, aber zugleich fliegen auch alle anderen Buchstaben des jeweiligen Wortes in den virtuellen Raum und formieren sich zu einer Wortskulptur, die im Raum herumflottiert. Die Buchstaben bilden einen Zugang (access) zum Speicher der Sprache. Hinter S verbergen sich soundso viele Wörter mit dem Anfangsbuchstaben S.

Angenommen, der Buchstabe S ist aktiviert. Dem Spaziergänger präsentiert sich jetzt z. B. das ‹Space› als räumliche Schleife S, der das Appendix ‹Space› (Schritt) aufgeprägt ist. Jedem der 26 Buchstaben sind diverse Wörter zugeordnet, die der Computerterminologie, der Sprache der Mathematik, der Physik oder der Philosophie entstammen (z. B.: ARBITARY, ALL, BINARY, IDENTITY, NOW, HERE, JUSTICE, DIDIT, FREEDOM, CODE, SYMBOL, ENTROPY etc.). Die veränderlichen Wortskulpturen machen das Wort fast immer unlesbar, indem sie seine Buchstaben plastisch ineinander und hintereinander geschichtet und gestapelt zur Erscheinung bringen. Auf die Bedeutung des Wortes beziehen sich – oftmals über etliche Transformationen – trotzdem viele Wortskulpturen: die Buchstabenfolge ist zwar unkenntlich, aber auf der Grundlage visuell dominanter Buchstaben wird die Bedeutung des Wortes plastisch. Die Wortskulpturen machen die Bedeutung zum Träger von Ähnlichkeit. Sie stellen eine Ähnlichkeit zwischen Buchstaben-Form und Bedeutung her und eine Unähnlichkeit, wenn das System ‹ungeordnet› reagiert. Das Wort ‹Scanning› wird als gescannte (geschichtete) Skulptur gezeigt. Die Semantik eines Wortes und die Physik eines Wortes, die immaterielle Bedeutung und die materielle Erscheinung eines Wortes werden selbstreferentiell rückgekoppelt.

Der Wortskulptur gesellt sich dann eine weitere hinzu, wenn ein zweiter Betrachter einen Kontaktpunkt aktiviert. Nach einer Weile entfalten beide Skulpturen sich zu linear lesbaren, sinnvollen Worten, die jetzt durch die Zeitwörter ‹is›, ‹has›, ‹seems› verknüpft werden. Zwei reale Subjekte auf der Tastatur des realen Bodens formieren damit einen virtuellen Satz, etwa: ‹identity is binary› oder ‹digit seems entropy›. Anschließend begeben sich die Wörter wieder in ihren Skulpturen-Status zurück, bevor sie sich dem Alphabet auf dem virtuellen Fußboden eingliedern. Es flottieren in der Text-Welt – neben dem Sinn – die Position, die Skalierung und die Rotation der

Skulpturen, je nach den Schritten des Betrachters über die 29 realen Bodentasten.

3. Die Raum-Welt

Die Welt des Raums und der Architektur, die Christian Möller nach einem Konzept von Peter Weibel ausgearbeitet und der Mathematiker Dieter Beck programmiert hat, geht von einem leeren, glatten, perspektivischen Innenraum aus. Sobald der virtuelle Raum über einen der farbigen Bodenpunkte betreten ist, brechen seine fünf glatten Flächen in sich selbst gleiche Teilelemente auf. Zehn verschiedenen Gruppierungen sind die Elemente der Raumflächen zugeordnet, die der Betrachter anschließend über die realen hellgrauen Bodenpunkte aktivieren kann. Sie stoßen dann mit unterschiedlicher Geschwindigkeit regelmäßig oder nach einem Zufallsalgorithmus in der aktivierten Gruppierung hervor, sodaß insgesamt 20 unterschiedliche Aufbrüche des Innenraums inszeniert werden können. Bewegt ist die Raum-Welt nur durch die einachsige Skalierung der Elemente, die oberflächig in kühlen Blau-Schwarz-Tönen hereinstoßen. Ihre Bewegung und Verteilung im Raum verläuft nach programmatischen Algorithmen, die – einmal aktiviert – sich selbst steuern. Dutzende Algorithmen machen den Raum in vielen Variationen selbst zum Bild des Raumes.
Kenntlich wird mit der Bewegung des Betrachters zunächst ein sich mit sich selbst einrichtender Raum: so können die divers skalierten Raumelemente vorübergehend wie aufgezogene Schubladen oder Schränke erscheinen. Die vom Computer unermüdlich deklinierte Inneneinrichtung der Raumsegmente führt unterschiedliche ästhetische Gebilde vor und suggeriert unterschiedliche ästhetische Erfahrungen. Der Eindruck des sich mit sich selbst einrichtenden Raums kann z. B. kurzfristig mit dem Eindruck einer nächtlichen Sky-Line wechseln. Diese architektonischen Assoziationen sind in der virtuellen Raum-Welt aber nur vorübergehend. Der aufbrechende, sich defor-

mierende Innenraum präsentiert sich nachhaltig und in erster Linie als Negativskulptur: als plastisches Gebilde, das sich mit der Bewegung des Betrachters aus den Flächen herauswölbt. Je länger und gründlicher man diesen virtuellen Raum vom realen Environment aus begeht, umso stärker wird der Eindruck eines sich mit unterschiedlicher Geschwindigkeit selbst zur Schau stellenden Raums. Ein selbstreferentieller Raum, der sich selbst als Objekt und Bild thematisiert. Die Wände selbst affiner bewegen sich, entfalten sich jenseits der Gravitation. Die dabei sich entfaltenden Erscheinungen können konkrete Formen wie von Inneneinrichtungen und abstrakte wie fraktale Raum-Module einnehmen. Der Betrachter gewinnt zunehmend das Gefühl, immer näher umgeben und umstellt zu werden. Je mehr er den Raum ergründet und begeht, umso gnadenloser kommt dieser Raum auf ihn zu. Der zunächst leere, dann aufbrechende Innenraum rückt ihm unausweichlich zu Leibe. Diese Raum-Welt hat einen zunächst ästhetischen, aber zunehmend unheimlichen Gesichtspunkt: sie kommt auf den Betrachter zu, ohne daß er sie ergründen könnte.

4. Die Objekt-Welt

Perspektive und Non-Identität der Gegenstände werden in der virtuellen Objekt-Welt (nach Konzepten von Peter Weibel von Akke Wagenaar designt und teilweise programmiert) nun konsequent in Szene gesetzt. Der Betrachter hat, wiederum über einen realen, farbigen Bodenpunkt, die Objekt-Welt betreten. Es erscheinen jetzt in schneller Kreuzbewegung und Rotation Objekte, die zunächst unkenntlich sind. Sie stoßen vor, kreuzen sich und rammen die Raumwände, wobei sie ihre Farbe und Textur gegen Farbe und Textur der Wände austauschen. In hoher Geschwindigkeit verändern sie ihre Skalierung, bevor sie sich schließlich zu erkennbaren Gebilden formieren. Sichtbar werden jetzt Stuhl, Tisch und Gesicht, so jedoch, daß von einem Stuhl, einem Tisch und einem Gesicht nicht die Rede sein kann.

Zu sehen ist vielmehr ein mit sechs Tischen fusionierter Stuhl, ein mit zwei Stühlen fusionierter Tisch und eine Gesichtsformation, die in der Mitte durch das eigene Profil gespalten ist: das flächig ausgezogene Spaltprofil reproduziert am anderen Ende der Spaltfläche Profil und Gesicht. Überdies wird das ausgezogene Spaltprofil seinerseits zweimal vom eigenen Double gespalten, so daß maximal fünf Gesichter bzw. Profile gleichzeitig sichtbar werden. Das Prinzip dieser Formation: die Spaltung des Gesichts durch das Pofil teilt nicht nur, sondern reproduziert auch das Gesicht.

Dieses erkennbare, doch irritierend gespaltene, doublierte und fusionierte Ensemble aus Tisch, Stuhl und Gesicht ist die Exposition der Objekt-Welt. Der Betrachter setzt sie in Gang, sobald er wieder die hellgrauen Bodenpunkte betritt. Mit ihnen aktiviert er die Rotation und perspektivische Deformation der Objekte um verschiedene Achsen sowie das Rammen gegen die Wände, den Austausch von Farbe und Textur zwischen Objekten und Raum, das gegenseitige Kreuzen der Objekte im Raum und ihre diverse Skalierung. Alle Aspekte der Erscheinungsweise der Dinge wie Proportion, Perspektive, Materialität, Farbe, Textur, Skalierung, Bewegung etc. werden vom Beobachter gesteuert. Je mehr er sich im realen Environment umherbewegt bzw. je mehr Betrachter die Kontaktpunkte betreten, umso verwirrender wird der Aspekt der Objekt-Welt.

Der von sechs Tischen durchdrungene Stuhl biegt, krümmt, zieht sich zurück und dehnt sich aus, der von zwei Stühlen durchdrungene Tisch windet, biegt und beugt sich und formiert sich vorübergehend auch zu einer (analytischen) Couch, der das gespaltene/doublierte Gesicht-Objekt nacheilt oder umkehrt. Der irritierende Aspekt dieses bewegten Ensembles aus ineinander verschmolzenen Gegenständen und gespalten/doubliertem Gesicht kulminiert in der Endphase des Programms, die sich nach einer vorgegebenen Zeit formiert. Die zuvor unkenntlichen Augen stoßen zum Schluß aus dem Gesicht hervor und zeichnen rote und grüne Strahlen. Sie

werden damit nicht als Augen, sondern quasi als Blick sichtbar.
Wie die abstrakte Architektur des Innenraums auf den Betrachter zukommt, stößt hier das Gesicht dem Betrachter als Blick zu und schaut ihn – gewissermaßen sichtbar – an. Dieser Gesichtspunkt des Objekts, das der Betrachter nicht einfach anschaut, sondern von dem er selbst angeschaut wird, irritiert seine Sicht bzw. den Rahmen seines Bildes erheblich. Konsequent erscheint ihm dann rückblickend die Veränderlichkeit des Bild- und Raumrahmens durch die rammenden Objekte. Die in ständiger Verzerrung flottierenden und rotierenden Objekte schwanken zwischen zwei Zuständen, nämlich zwischen weichen Zeichenzuständen und harten Dingzuständen, zwischen der Welt der Sprache und der Welt der Architektur, zwischen Semantik und Physik. Das gespaltene Subjekt (das Gesichtsobjekt) überträgt seine eigene Nichtidentität (denn die Schizo-Spaltung ist die Voraussetzung des Subjekts) auf die Welt der Objekte.

Susanne Craemer
On Justifying the Hypothetical Nature of Art and the Non-Identicality within the Object World

An interactive computer installation by Peter Weibel at the Gallery Tanja Grunert, Cologne, 5. June – 1. August 1992

1. The Installation

The visitor is received into a completely dark, acute-angled triangular space of aluminium plates on a steel-girder construction. The only source of light comes from a screen measuring 5 x 3,75 m. It constitutes the open (transparent) and of a real environment which will present other, virtual worlds. The ground plan (by architect Christian Möller) for the environment is based on the front elevation of the saddle-roof type of house common in these regions and known as ‹St. Nicolas' House›. The screen is found at the ‹left hand side of the roof-slant› on which images fall via back projection from a wide-screen CAD data-projector.
The visitor will start the game as he moves into the dark space. As soon as he has touched the floor perforated by grey and coloured spots he has to make up his mind: either he stays firmly rooted in reality – if he avoids the coloured spots – or he takes a

plunge from the real environment into a virtual one by stepping onto one of the red, green or blue spots on the floor. By taking such a step he chooses one of various possible virtual worlds; by subsequently stepping on the remaining light-grey spots on the floor-mat he can navigate through his chosen virtual world and the perceptive experiences it proffers. In effect the visitor is able to leap backwards and forwards between virtual and real world, as well as several virtual worlds. Once he has stepped into a particular world-mode he can control its appearance, and the shapes and apparitions in it by continuing to walk on the light grey floor points. Thus he selects not only the codes for the various ‹world-modes›, but also plays around with the modules of these codes as he progresses. His steps will evoke changing images of these worlds that are projected in real time on the huge screen.
What are the prerequisites for these concrete images, this walk in leaps and bounds through virtual worlds provided in real time?
First, the floor, the active area of the installation, has been underlayed with a number of sensors marked on the surface: stepping on a red, green, or blue spot activates one of three virtual worlds; stepping on the remaining 29 light grey spots scattered throughout the room activates the shapes in, and appearance of each respective world on the screen. The technical operation is as follows: the sensors, individual contact mats, determine the visitor's presence and absence which they transmit to a circuit board (constructed by Bob O'Kane) which controls 32 switches in a button-box which correspond to the 32 contact-mats. The received information, in accordance with programmes initially selected by activating the coloured sensors, triggers numerical operations and algorithms in a computer (Silicon Graphics 4D/320 VGX) connected to the system. This digitally coded information is now transformed into graphic (visual) information and fed to a data-projector generating images in real time through video back projection on the large screen. Gideon

May has co-ordinated the programmes for the respective virtual words so, that once activated by the various real floor sensors, they can be manifested consecutively in one shared virtual space of the screen. Thus the installation presents itself in three parts:
1. Solid reality of the floor perforated by three coloured and 29 light grey spots which invite the ambling visitor to plunge into various virtual worlds.
2. The circuitry connecting these interfaces to the programmes determining the various worlds.
3. The images screened in video back projection reacting to the visitor directly and in real time.

Via the interfaces in the floor the installation reacts directly and interactively to the user. However, as opposed to his situation when facing the alphabetic keyboard of a typewriter, for instance, the user is unable to operate the 32 floor sensors instrumentally. Instead, he himself is being sensed by the alphabetically arranged keys of the floor contacts. The observer is being perceived by the sensors of a huge typewriter, subsequently interpreted by the computer, and represented on screen. The observer himself is turned into a tool. This device, which perverts the instrumental function of conventional writing systems nevertheless constitutes an interface which, with its 32 floor keys (3 world-modes, 26 letters, 3 additional signs) is organized like language, in that it transmits not the message, but the presence of a subject, thus not re-presenting reality, but presenting the conditions for the construction of that reality.

Thus the three virtual worlds available to the visitor via red, green, or blue spot-activation reveal in a most unusual way to our manifest experience our own distorted perception of reality. The three available worlds are the world of text, the world of space, and the world of objects. The observer can skip from one to the other. By activating one of the coloured sensors you can enter one of three possible virtual worlds, where green corresponds to the text-world, red to the world of objects, and blue the world of space. The next 29 light grey sensors then only trigger

the transformations in each chosen world, so long as no other colour-key is stepped on. Each time you step on a new colour point a different virtual world will appear.
To describe the three worlds perceived as undergoing constant deformation and movement before their interaction with the observer you would see the following:
– an empty interior space (spatial world)
– alphabetical letters, words, whole sentences (text world)
– a table, a chair, a human face (object world)
An interior with a subject, a table and chair, where a conversation is taking place is part of our most common daily experience. The three world-modes radically disrupt the triviality of such a common experience: in these virtual worlds our familiar reality of a room with a table and chair, human faces and coherent words and phrases appears only – if at all – as lingering image. The world of reliable, constant phenomena is transformed into a world of variables. Familiar conceptions of identity and reality, the distinction between subject and object are thus put into question. Non-identity and incommensurability are becoming axiomatic. In these worlds, space, objects, and text can be moved and transformed beyond recognition by the observer following these parameters: the position of the elements in these worlds may be transmuted and moved along the coordinate axes X, Y, Z by the observer changing their scale, proportion, and rotation. In addition, the observer can also control certain extra functions: twirl, twist, and wave functions, textures between objects are transformed (real texture of objects changing into numerical digits, letters etc. as texture), texture can be moved between objects and wall; just as in a thermodynamic system the energy-level remains constant, so that movement may be transferred from one object to another; instead of texture we may well occasionally obtain twisted ribbon models as movement leaves behind its trace when the overdraw function is in operation, the aggregate condition of phenomena changes into opaque shapes or twisted ribbon models, dots or lines etc.

Thus space, text, and objects may do ‹things› and obey laws which definitely contravene those of our daily experience. Here, their properties may be borrowed from each other. Words become material and spatial, objects take on the texture of letters, and space may break-up into several self-identical objects. In their respective cross-referentiality and through the distortion of its usual appearance by changing just a few of its parameters these virtual worlds thus demonstrate more precisely how they are shattering our usual everyday perception of reality.

2. The Text-World

The visitor has now stepped onto a colour-point and is immersed in the world of language. The Text-World designed by Constanze Ruhm after original draughts by Peter Weibel (programmes devised by Bob O'Kane) presents a virtual space on the screen on whose floor we find the letters of the alphabet arranged as on a keyboard. Now the observer in the real environment moves on, or someone else steps onto one of the light grey points of contact connected to the 26 letters of the alphabet. Once activated, a letter in the virtual space takes off from the floor, leaving back his double; but at the same time all other letters of a particular word take off into virtual space where they combine into a word sculpture floating freely in space. The letters provide access to the language store. For example, we have so and so many words beginning with an S behind the letter S. If S is activated, the visitor will, for example, be presented with ‹Space› as a spatial, S-shaped curvature overlayed with the appendix word ‹Space›. Various words taken from computer terminology, mathematics, physics, or philosophy have been assigned to each of the 26 letters (e.g. ARBITRARY, ALL, BINARY, IDENTITY, NOW, HERE, JUSTICE, DIGIT, FREEDOM, CODE, SYMBOL, ENTROPY, e.t.c.). These transmutable word sculptures almost always render the word itself illegible by displaying its constituent letters spatially intertwined, layered, or piled-up on top of each other. Nevertheless, many of the sculptures will refer back – via several transformations – to the meaning of the selected word: The correct order of letters having become unrecognizable, a word's significance will nonetheless appear plastically evident on the basis of individual, visually dominant letters. These word sculptures reveal significance as bearer of associative similarities. They create similarities between a letter's shape and its meaning, and dissimilarities when the system is reacting in a ‹disorderly› fashion. Hence the word ‹scanning› would be shown as a scanned sculpture. A self-referential feed-back effect links the semantics and physics of a word, its immaterial significance and its material appearance.

When a second observer activates a contact-point the word sculpture will be joined by another one. After a while, both sculptures develop into linear, legible, comprehensible words which are then linked through such verbs as ‹is›, ‹has›, ‹seems›. Thus, two real subjects acting on the keyboard of the real floor have formed a virtual sentence such as ‹identity is binary› or ‹digit seems entropy›. Thereafter the words return to their status as sculpture, before re-joining the alphabet on the virtual floor. In the Text-World, besides meaning – position, scale, and rotation of the sculptures are thus floating freely, depending on the steps taken by the observer on the 29 real keys on the floor.

3. The Space-World

The world of space and architecture (devised by Christian Möller after an original concept by Peter Weibel and programmed by Dieter Beck) is based on an empty, smooth, interior space complying to the rules of linear perspective. As soon as you enter virtual space via one of the coloured floor-points its five constituent smooth planes break up into self-identical segments. These planar spatial elements have been assigned to ten different possible groups of combinations which the observer may activate via the light grey floor-points. These erupt regularly but with different speeds, or combine in accordance with an incidental algorithm so that eventually 20 different new spatial configurations may be enacted. Movement occurs only by means of scaling the individual elements, marked in cool hues of black and blue, along one axis. Their movement and dispersal in space is controlled by programmatic algorithms which are, once activated, self-regulatory. Dozens of algorithms transform space itself in its many variations into an image of space.

As he moves on, the observer initially glimpses a self-furnishing interior setting itself up from its own constituents: the various, differently scaled, spatial elements temporarily appear seemingly as opened drawers or a cupboard. The incessant declension of spatial segments into continually changing interiors by the computer will generate various aesthetic formations evoking all sorts of aesthetic experiences. Thus the impression of a self-furnishing interior may briefly give way to that of an urban skyline by night. However, in the virtual Space-World these associative architectural impressions are but fleeting. An interior continually breaking up and deformed will primarily present itself as negative sculpture: a sculptural formation bulging from the planar expanses according to how the observer is moving. As you explore this virtual space from your position in real space longer and more thoroughly, the impression gained is one of a room under pretentious self-display at different speeds, a self-referential space articulating itself as object and image. Walls move and erect themselves beyond gravity. The resulting manifestations may take the form of concrete, familiar shapes such as interior room furniture, as well as abstract, fractal spatial modules. Increasingly, the observer gains the impression of being surrounded and confined. The further he explores the space, the more mercilessly the latter will close-in on him. There is no physical escape from this once empty and subsequently broken-up interior. What initially had aesthetic appeal is turning increasingly sinister: the Space-World is closing-in on the observer without him being able to really come to grips with it.

4. The Object-World

In the virtual world of objects (designed and part-programmed by Akke Wagenaar after original concepts by Peter Weibel) their perspective and nonidentity are consequently revealed. Again the observer has entered the Object-World via a real, coloured floor-point. Now fast-moving and rotating objects that are at first unfamiliar cross the screen. They advance, crossing each others' paths, and collide with the walls of the space, exchanging their own colour and texture for that of the wall. They change scale rapidly, before mutating into discernible shapes. Now a chair, table, and a face will appear, but looking quite unlike what you consider they should be like. Instead we glimpse a chair fused to six tables, a table fusing with two chairs and some facial expression split in the middle by its own profile: that profile then stretched flat reproduces both profile and face on the other end of the split apparition. The stretch profile itself is split down further, twice, by its own double, so that now a maximum of five faces or profiles appear simultaneously. The principle behind this formation: splitting-up the face will not only subdivide, but also reproduce the face.

This recognizable but irritatingly split, doubled, and fused ensemble of table, chair, and human face exposes the Object-World. As soon as he steps on the light grey floor-points the observer will set it off. He is now activating the rotation and perspective deformation of the objects around several axes, as well as controlling their collisions with the walls, the exchange of colour and texture between objects and walls, and the various scales and courses of the crossing paths of their trajectories. All the aspects of the objects' appearance like proportion, perspective position, materiality, colour, and texture can thus be controlled by the observer. As he continues to move in his real environment, and as more and more observers will tread on the contact-points, so the impression of the Object-World will get increasingly confused.

The chair pierced by six tables warps, bends, withdraws, and expands; the table pierced by two chairs twists, bends, and bows, then temporarily changes into a(n) (analyst's) couch in hot pursuit of the split/doubled) facial object or vice versa.

The irritating visions of this fast-moving ensemble of objects fused to one another and split/doubled facial expressions reaches its climax during the final phase of the programme taking effect after a given time. The eyes, so far uncharacteristic, suddenly burst out from the face, emitting red and green beams. Hereby they are made apparent not so much as eyes, but as quasi-gaze.

In the same way as the abstract architecture of the interior was advancing on the spectator, the spectacle of the human face now collides with the observer's gaze, its sight clearly meeting his gaze. The object's vision which is not simply being observed by the spectator, but is clearly looking back on him, seriously irritates our vision and the framework for our image. To the observer the transformation of the image-frame or the borders of the space by the colliding objects now seems consequential in retrospect. The floating, rotating, and continually distorted objects are veering between two states: the soft state of signs, and the hard state of objects, they veer between the world of language and the world of architecture, semantics and physics. The split subject (the facial object) is applying its own nonidentity to the world of objects (as the schizoid split provides the basis for the subject).

Robert Fleck
Peter Weibel – Concept Art und Wiener Aktionismus

Im Jahre 1967 realisierte Peter Weibel eine für seine künstlerische Arbeit zentrale Aktion. Bei ‹ZOCK-Exercises›, einem der ersten Kollektivhappenings des Wiener Aktionismus, tippte er mit durch Zeitungsausschnitte verbundenen Augen einen Vortrag in eine alte mechanische Schreibmaschine, ohne das ‹Blindschreibsystem› zu beherrschen. Das Ergebnis dieser von der Maschine bei Weibels verklebten Augen gesteuerten Niederschrift trug Weibel dann wortgetreu vor. Gegenstand des Vortrages, der den Titel ‹Zock antwortet wohl› trug, war im weitesten Sinne das Verhältnis von Kunst und Denken. Die Technologie als ein autonomes, den beiden anderen gleichwertiges Medium hatte sich in diese beiden Kategorien vermittelnd integriert.

Diese Arbeit kann als Schlüsselwerk für Peter Weibel angesehen werden. Nicht zuletzt mit diesem Event gewann der damals in der Wiener Szene bereits als junger Künstler und Kunsttheoretiker bekannte Weibel auch Profil. Es war kein Zufall, daß dies im Rahmen des Wiener Aktionismus stattfand, und zwar bei einem der ersten Auftritte einer Bewegung, die unter dem Namen ‹ZOCK› ab Ende 1966 als die öffentlichkeitszugewandte Phase des Wiener Aktionismus den Versuch einer Kulturrevolution in Österreich einleitete. Peter Weibel aber gelangte mit seiner Aktion in den Status eines authentischen Nachfolgers des Wiener Aktionismus in besonderen, neuerschlossenen Bereichen wie den Medien und ihrer Technologie. Es ist dies auch eine Position, die Weibels Werk bis heute charakterisiert.

Genauer betrachtet, hat Weibels damalige Arbeit vornehmlich mit drei Momenten zu tun, die auch Weibels heutige Arbeit prägen. Zum einen befinden wir uns an einer Schnittstelle von Aktionskunst und konzeptioneller Arbeit, wie sie in der amerikanischen Kunst dieser Zeit die frühe Body Art repräsentiert. Nirgendwo wird dies deutlicher als im Vergleich von Weibels Event von 1967 mit den anderen Aktionen des gleichen Happenings. Bei ‹ZOCK-Exercises›, am 17. April 1967 in der Wiener Galerie nächst St. Stephan veranstaltet, trugen Hauptprotagonisten des Wiener Aktionismus wie Otto Mühl und Hermann Nitsch Events vor, die deutlicherweise aus einer zur realen Aktion gesteigerten neoexpressionistischen Malerei kamen, wie sie die Wurzel und das Kennzeichen des klassischen Wiener Aktionismus war. Mühl warf und schleuderte mit Bettfedern herum und operierte, auf einem Podest stehend, mit mehreren entrollten Rollen Toilettenpapieres. Nitsch zog einen mit Wasser gefüllten Plastiksack, zwischen den Besuchern hin und hergehend, an einer Schnur hinter sich her. Und der Schriftsteller und Philosoph Oswald Wiener, die dominierende Gestalt unter jenen Wiener Literaten, die unter dem Namen ‹Literarisches Cabaret›, später als ‹Wiener Gruppe›, Ende der fünfziger Jahre als erste happeningähnliche Aufführungsformen in Wien eingeführt hatten, hielt vor der österreichischen Staatsflagge stehend einen anarchistischen Vortrag per Megaphon.

Weibels weit stillere, aber sehr innovative und vom Publikum damals als Skandal aufgenommene Aktion partizipierte durchaus an diesen beiden Seiten der damaligen Wiener Aktionskunst, verschob jedoch ihre Koordinaten. Der Event war gewiß sehr körperlich. Weibels Körper war Gegenstand wie Träger des Werkes, und zwar durchaus – im Sinne des Wiener Aktionismus – als ein hysterischer, aufgeladener Körper (Gilles Deleuze). Doch wurde der Körper in Weibels Aktion, anders als im klassischen Wiener Aktionismus, nicht mehr nach dem Vorbild des Malers beim Malakt und damit als gestenreicher, hyperaktiver Akteur eingesetzt. Sondern er wurde selbst als Form, als Einheit begriffen und als Medium verstanden. Genau dies verbindet Weibels Event mit den frühen Zeugnissen der Body Art.

Zugleich war Weibels Arbeit bei diesem Happening, anders als die Arbeiten der Wiener Aktionisten und auch Oswald Wieners, durchgehend konzeptuell. Das Realisat war bei Mühl etwa das von Provokationen begleitete aktionistische ‹Malen› mit Bettfedern und Toilettenpapier. Dieses von den Wiener Aktionisten entwickelte formale Vokabular kehrte Weibel dagegen ins Konzept. Das Realisat in Weibels Aktion lag allein im Denken. Nicht der durch die verselbständigte Schreibmaschine ‹gestörte› und realisierte Vortrag war das Werk, sondern ein Prozeß, in dem Sehen und Denken ein dialogisches Kontinuum ergaben, das sich um eine konkrete Technologie drehte, wobei dies durch die Verwendung des reduziertestmöglichen Formenvokabulars in seiner allein mentalen Realität erhalten war. Dies unterschied Peter Weibel damals von den Wiener Aktionisten ebenso wie von den mit Oswald Wiener ins Happening eingestiegenen Literaten. Es verband ihn aber umsomehr mit der Innovation und dem Wesen der damals gerade entstehenden konzeptuellen Kunst.

Als zweites Moment in Weibels Arbeit von 1967 sticht ein spezifisches Thema hervor, das zum allgemeinen Charakteristikum der zumeist aus dem Wiener Aktionismus heraus entstandenen österreichischen Variante der Concept Art werden sollte. Es ist jenes eines Herangehens an die Idee einer das Sehen und das Denken ohne Vermittlung kurzschließenden Kunst, wie es die Idee der Concept Art war, über das Mittel der ‹Sprachkritik›. Diese war die wesentliche Leistung der modernen Philosophie in Österreich und als solche natürlicherweise verfügbar. Alle

Protagonisten der Concept Art in Österreich stützten sich später in zentraler Weise auf dieses Instrument, wobei Weibel, der gerade in diesen Jahren durch Aufenthalte in Paris den dortigen Strukturalismus in seine Arbeit integrierte, dies neben Oswald Wiener zuallererst in Wien einführte.
Aufgrund einer durchgängig anti-hegelianischen, zugleich aber pro-kantianischen Tradition der philosophischen Moderne in Österreich seit dem frühen 19. Jahrhundert war die zunächst von Ernst Mach und dann von den führenden Wiener Philosophen der Jahre 1910 bis 1930, Ludwig Wittgenstein und dem ‹Wiener Kreis›, entwickelte philosophische Methodik zum einen von einem radikal anti-metaphysischen und anti-ideologischen Ansatz gespeist und zum anderen an einer konkreten Methodik solcher Anti-Ideologie interessiert. Die Idee, Zeichen- und Bedeutungssysteme allein von innen her, immanent in ihrer eigenen Gesetzlichkeit zu begreifen und sie auf Fehlerstellen hin abzutasten, war dessen logische Folge und macht auch die Wiener Methode der ‹Sprachkritik› aus, wie sie bei dem frühen und dem späten, exilierten Wittgenstein ebenso erscheint wie beim dogmatischeren ‹Sinnkriterium› des ‹Wiener Kreises› und dem späteren ‹Falsifikationskriterium› von Karl Popper gleichfalls im englischen Exil. Als Wiener bildende Künstler, allen voran Weibel, sich in den späteren sechziger Jahren auf das Unterfangen der Concept Art, jenes einer möglichst unmittelbar mit dem Denken verbundenen visuellen Kunst, einließen, griffen sie natürlicherweise dieses Instrument auf.
In der geschilderten konzeptuellen Aktion von Peter Weibel trat diese ‹sprachkritische› Seite der aus Österreich kommenden Konzeptkunst früh hervor. Nicht das im Vortrag Angesprochene war Gegenstand der Aktion, sondern die Entkleidung und praktische Erprobung des dazu führenden Systems. In diesem Sinn ‹dekonstruierte› Peter Weibel in dem kleinen Event ‹ZOCK-Exercises› auf sprachkritische Weise ein ganzes technologisches System. Er betrat damit ein Feld, das bis heute das Zentrum bildet, um das seine Installationen und Performances kreisen.

Dies aber führt uns auch zum dritten entscheidenden Moment von Weibels Arbeit und zugleich zu Weibels entscheidender Innovation. Sie besteht in der engen Verbindung von Concept Art und Mediensprache beziehungsweise von Technologie. Anders als die meisten anderen Vertreter der frühen Concept Art stützte Weibel sich ja nicht in erster Linie auf die visuellen Potentiale der Sprache oder des menschlichen Körpers, sondern, beides verknüpfend, auf jenes der Technologie. Schon 1967 verband diese die beiden Momente, den konzeptuell eingesetzten Körper und die Schreibmaschine, die das Werk zugleich produzierte und sein Thema war. Weibels Begegnung mit dem französischen Strukturalismus und mit dem Situationismus mit ihrer beiderseitigen Medienkritik bei seinen Aufenthalten in Paris spielt als Einfluß auf diesen Innovationsschritt, der den technologischen Zweig der Concept Art mitbegründete, eine unleugbare Rolle.
Die seitherige Entwicklung der Kunst von Peter Weibel kann damit zusammengefaßt werden, daß Weibel diesen dreigliedrigen Ansatz durchhielt und ausbaute. Ein Körpereinsatz im Sinn der Body Art, die Sprachkritik als formales Instrument und die Technologie als zentrales, beide verbindendes Thema definiert gerade auch Weibels Werk der achtziger und beginnenden neunziger Jahre, insbesondere die Arbeit mit Video, die für Weibel bald nach dem Event von 1967 begann. Was sich gegenüber der Arbeit von 1967 gewandelt hat, ist zum einen die Grundlage der zeitgenössischen Technologie, die Weibel sprachkritisch untersucht. Die Wandlung von der Technologie der Schreibmaschine zu jener des fortgeschrittenen Computers kongenial umgesetzt zu haben, macht heute Weibels Stellung aus. Diese Wandlung, die in Verbindung mit Video hochkomplexe, automatisierte Systeme virtueller Realität voraussetzt, erzwang zum anderen gegenüber den frühen Werken Weibels einen Schritt, den auch die meisten anderen Vertreter der frühen konzeptuellen Body Art auf bestimmte Weise gingen. Der Event, den Weibels heutige Installationen produzieren, ist nach

wie vor auf dem konzeptuell eingesetzten Körper und der visuellen Sprachkritik von Bedeutungssystemen aufgebaut, wobei die Technologie beides verbindet. Der Körper aber, um den es sich in den heutigen Arbeiten Weibels handelt, ist jener des Betrachters, der gewissermaßen die Stellung einnimmt, die Weibel in der frühen Aktion von 1967 noch selbst auf sich nahm. Der Betrachter vollzieht nunmehr die visuelle und zugleich ‹aktionistische› Sprachkritik der Systeme virtueller Realität. Konzeptuelle Body Art in diesem Sinne allein auf der Technologie aufzubauen, bleibt, wie früher, das Kennzeichen der Kunst von Peter Weibel, der damit die Herausforderung durchstand, eine authentische Nachfolge des Wiener Aktionismus der sechziger Jahre anzutreten. Doch tritt ein Zug, der in der Aktion von 1967 nur angelegt war, heute bei Weibel deutlich hervor, jener nämlich, gegenüber den archaisierenden Tendenzen des Wiener Aktionismus eine entscheidende Verlagerung und Öffnung hin zur postindustriellen Zivilisation vollzogen zu haben.

Robert Fleck
Peter Weibel – Concept Art and Wiener Aktionismus

In the year 1967, Peter Weibel performed what for his artistic work was a crucial action. At ‹ZOCK-Exercises›, one of the first collective happenings of Vienna Action Art, Weibel – with his eyes bound shut by newspaper clippings – typed a lecture on an old mechanical typewriter without ever having learned to touch-type ‹blind›. He then pulled the text from the machine and read it aloud word for word. The object of this lecture with the title ‹Zock Does Answer› was, in broadest terms, that of art and thought. Technology, as an autonomous medium on equal footing with the other two, was integrated as mediator.

This can be seen as a key of Peter Weibel. Not least of all because of this performance, Weibel – already known as a young artist and art theorist of the Viennese scene – gained general recognition. It was no accident that this took place within the first framework of Vienna Action Art and during one of the first appearances of this movement that from the end of 1966 under the name of ZOCK led to its public phase and the attempt at a cultural revolution in Austria. With this action Peter Weibel achieved the status of an authentic successor to Vienna Action Art, specifically in the newly accessible field of the media and their technology. This is a position that characterizes Weibel and his work still today.

When examined more closely, it becomes clear, that Weibel's work at the time dealt with three aspects that still apply to what he is presently doing. First, we find ourselves at the seamline between Action Art and Concept Art as represented in the early Body Art of the time in America. This is nowhere more apparent than a comparison between Weibel's event of 1967 and the other actions at the same Happening. ZOCK-Exercises were staged on 17 April 1967 in the Wiener Galerie next to St. Stephan's. Some of Vienna Action Art's main protagonists, like Otto Mühl and Hermann Nitsch, carried out performances that clearly stemmed from a heightened form of neo-expressionistic painting into-action, as Mühl whirled and slung around bed feathers and manipulated several unravelled rolls of toilet paper while standing on a rostrum. Nitsch dragged behind him on a string a plastic sack filled with water, walking to and fro between the members of the audience. The writer and philosopher Oswald Wiener was there as the commanding figure among those Viennese literati known as the ‹Literary Cabaret› and later as the ‹Wiener Gruppe› (Vienna as well as Wiener Group); at the end of the Fifties he had introduced the first happening-like form of performance art to Vienna. That evening in 1967 he stood before an Austrian flag and intoned an anarchist speech through a megaphone.

Weibel's much quieter but very innovative action, regarded by the audience as scandalous, included the two sides of Vienna Action Art at the time, but shifted its coordinates. The action was certainly very physical. Weibel's body was object and vehicle of the work, a body thoroughly in keeping with the spirit of Vienna Action Art, namely, hysterically charged (Gilles Deleuze). But the body in Weibel's action, in contrast to classical Vienna Actionism, was no longer a model for the artist himself in the act of painting, i.e., no longer a gesturing, hyperactive actor. It was seen as a form in itself, a unit and a medium. It is exactly here that Weibel's action is linked to the early events in Body Art.

At the same time, Weibel's work at this Happening, in contrast to the works of the Vienna Actionists and also to Oswald Wiener, was conceptual. The final realization for Mühl was the act of ‹painting› with bed feathers and toilet paper accompanied by audience provocation. The formal vocabulary thus developed by the Vienna Actionists Weibel now transformed into concept. The final realization in Weibel's action was alone that of thought. It was not the lecture (realized and ‹impeded› by the indifferent typewriter), but the process itself, based on a concrete technique where the acts of seeing and thinking came together in a dialogic continuum. And in so doing, this process was preserved in all its mental reality with the use of the most reductionist of formal vocabularies. This differentiated Peter Weibel from the Vienna Actionists of the time as well as from the literati who, with Oswald Wiener, turned to Happenings. This linked Weibel all the more to the innovation and the essence of the newly emerging conceptual art of the time.

As a second aspect of Weibel's work of 1967, one specific theme stands out, which was to become a general characteristic of the Austrian variant of Concept Art that for the most part evolved from Vienna Action Art. The idea behind Concept Art was to approach the theme of seeing and thinking without art being there to mediate and to short-circuit, but rather with the medium of a critique of language. This was Austria's essential contribution to modern philosophy and, as such, generally available. All of the Concept Art protagonists in Austria later used this crucial tool as a foundation to build on, whereby Weibel, who also integrated into his work the structuralism that he brought back from stays in Paris, was – together with Oswald Wiener – the first to introduce it to Vienna.

Based on the general anti-Hegelian but pro-Kantian tradition of modern philosophy in Austria since the early 19th century, philosophic methodology evolved first out of Ernst Mach and then out of the leading Viennese philosophers of the time between 1910 and 1930, Ludwig Wittgenstein, and the Vienna circle and was, on the one hand, fed by a radical anti-metaphysical and anti-ideological approach and, on the other, interested in concrete methods for such anti-ideology. The logical conclusion to this was that sign and meaning systems can be grasped solely from the inside according to their own immanent legitimacy and can be probed for sources of error; this concept is what distinguishes the Vienna method's critique of language as it occurs during the early and late exiles of Wittgenstein, as well as in the ‹criterion of meaningfulness› of the Vienna circle and the later ‹criterion of falsification› of Karl Popper, also exiled in England. When artists from Vienna (above all Weibel), parallel to the late Sixties' ventures of Concept Art, became engaged in a visual art linked as closely to thought as possible, they naturally took this up as an instrument.

The ‹language critique› side of Austrian Concept Art turned up very early in the 1967 action of Peter Weibel. The contents of the lecture was not its object, but the uncovering and practical testing of the system leading to the lecture. In this sense Peter Weibel's action in ‹ZOCK-Exercises› deconstructed a whole technological system by means of a critique of language. He thus entered the field that still today is the center around which his installations and performances turn.

This, then, leads us to the third decisive aspect of Weibel's work and at the same time to his decisive innovation: the link between Concept Art and media-language, i.e., technology. In early Concept Art Weibel did not, for the most part, base his themes on the visual potential of language or on the human body but – linking them together – on technology. As early as 1967 these two moments intermingled – the conceptually implemented body and language – in the then timely form of the mechanical typewriter, which produced the work and, at the same time, was its theme. Weibel's Paris encounter with French structuralism and situationism, with their dual criticism of the media, played an undeniable role in influencing his innovative stroke that helped found the technological arm of Concept Art.

How Peter Weibel's art then evolved can be summed up by saying that Weibel maintained and extended this three-tiered approach. The use of the body with Body Art intention, the critique of language as formal instrument and technology as a central theme, linking the two defines well with Weibel's work in the Eighties and the beginning of the Nineties, above all with his video work that began soon after the ZOCK action in 1967. What has changed since 1967 is, for one, the basis for contemporary technology that Weibel analyzes linguistically. To have aptly shifted his emphasis from the technology of the typewriter to that of advanced computers is what goes to establish Weibel's status today. Secondly, this shift, which in connection with video requires highly complex automatic systems of virtual reality, necessitated a move forward from Weibel's early works, a move which most of the other representatives of early conceptual Body Art took in their own way. The event that Weibel's present installations produce is still built on the conceptually manipulated human body and the visual linguistic critique of meaning systems, whereby technology is the link between the two. The body in question in Weibel's work here, however, is the viewer's own, which so to speak stands in for that of Weibel in the early 1967 action. The viewer himself consumates the visual and simultaneously ‹actionist› linguistic criticism directed against virtual-reality systems. To construct a conceptual body in this sense on technology alone remains as ever a trademark of Peter Weibel's art, who has thus survived as an authentic successor to Vienna Action Art of the Sixties. But today a characteristic comes to light very clearly that was only touched on in the 1967 action. Namely, in comparison to the archaic tendencies of Vienna Actionism, Weibel has effected a decisive turn toward, and an opening to, post-industrial civilization.

Translated from the German by Jeanne Haunschild

Hubert Damisch
Six notes et quelques questions pour une phénoménologie des images dites ‹virtuelles›

1. C'est chose désormais avérée: on n'en a décidément pas fini avec la perspective. Au moins la perspective qui était censée être celle des peintres, la *perspectiva artificialis*, dans sa différence avec la *perspectiva naturalis* à quoi se résumait l'optique traditionelle, antique et médiévale. Cette même perspective, dite encore ‹scientifique›, qui a fait son apparition, au Quattrocento, dans le champ qui était alors celui de la peinture, pour s'imposer bientôt comme le paradigme par excellence du système de la représentation classique, et dont la vulgate moderniste a voulu que le temps, la fortune, le rôle historique soient venus à leur terme avec Cézanne et le Cubisme. Le paradoxe étant que par le biais de la photographie, du cinéma, et celui, désormais, des images dites de synthèse, aucune époque n'aura été aussi massivement *informée* que la nôtre par un dispositif qui relève de toute évidence d'une autre forme d'histoire que strictement régionale et évolutionniste: une histoire ‹verticale› comme la nommait Merleau-Ponty, et qui prête, en tant que telle, à accumulation et à sédimentation, ainsi qu'il en va pour l'histoire des sciences ou de la philosophie, avec tous les effets d'enfouissement, mais aussi bien d'affleurement, de déplacement, de rema-

niement, d'interférence, de télescopage, toutes les possibilités, les occasions, les propositions de fouille, d'exhumation, voire d'*invention*, qui confèrent à cette histoire une dimension proprement archéologique.
La perspective, chose du passé? Le fait est qu'il est à présent impossible d'en parler plus longtemps comme d'une formation idéologique périmée et caduque: l'outil tout ensemble théorique et pratique, conceptuel et instrumental, spéculatif et utilitaire qu'elle représente, dans tous les sens du mot, cet outil a en effet retrouvé droit de cité dans le champ des images de synthèse et des espaces, des environnements déclarés ‹virtuels›. Que dans leur principe, leur mode d'engendrement, leur fonctionnement réglé, et jusqu'aux expériences auxquelles elles prêtent de la part des concepteurs autant que des usagers, les techniques de simulation mises en œuvre dans ce champ impliquent à terme un profond remaniement du dispositif de la représentation ne change rien à l'affaire: le modèle perspectif n'en est pas moins toujours au travail, dans des limites précises, et sous des espèces certes nouvelles, mais qui n'en manifestent que mieux, par différence, sa pertinence et son utilité. Sans doute peut-on travailler à son ‹dépassement›, mais par les moyens encore qui sont, au moins pour partie, les siens. La question étant précisément de déterminer dans quelle mesure, et *jusqu'à quel point* le modèle perspectif est à même d'instruire son propre procès, d'œuvrer à son propre dépassement ou, à tout le moins, de le réguler.
2. La réponse qu'on pourra être tenté de donner à cette question variera selon qu'on s'en tiendra à une caractérisation strictement idélogique de la *perspectiva artificialis* ou qu'on y reconnaîtra un paradigme dont on ne saurait se débarrasser facilement dès lors qu'il propose l'image la plus claire et la plus cohérente du dispositif qui peut être celui de la représentation, en même temps qu'il en constitue l'outil le plus efficace. Quel qu'en soit le domaine d'application, les techniques de simulation empruntent moins de la géométrie projective que de la per-

spective au sens le plus conventionnel du terme: et comment en irait-il autrement, dès lors que le sujet, ou comme on voudra dire, l'usager, l'observateur, celui qu'on nommait au siècle classique le *regardant*, y est par principe impliqué, et que si *projection* il y a et doit y avoir, elle n'a de sens qu'à s'ordonner à un point défini comme celui de l'œil, ou du sujet (*il punto dell-'occhio, der Augenpunkt*), et qui ne fait qu'un, projectivement parlant avec le point dit de fuite qui en est l'image sur le plan de projection? Avec pour conséquence que les premiers appareils conçus pour offrir à l'usager une image en perspective qui irait se modifiant et se transformant en fonction des mouvements de sa tête, voire de son corps, aient explicitement renoué avec le modèle albertien: le problème étant, à ce stade, de concevoir un dispositif tel que soient immédiatement éliminés les traits qui, suite à un déplacement ou un changement d'orientation de la ‹fenêtre›, ne trouveraient plus à s'inscrire dans le cadre à travers lequel le spectacle serait donné à voir, et que puissent au contraire y entrer tous ceux qui demeuraient auparavant en dehors du champ visuel.

3. Si différence il y a entre une vue en perspective construite sur le plan à deux dimensions du mur ou du tableau et un espace artificiel, visualisé à l'aide de techniques de synthèse d'images, elle correspondrait d'abord à une différence de régime: là où l'expérience fondatrice à laquelle s'attache le nom de Brunelleschi supposait que l'observateur appliquât un œil, et un seul, au revers du panneau percé d'un trou sur lequel était peint le baptistère de Florence pour le considérer au miroir (la perspective ayant ainsi partie liée, dès l'origine, avec l'image *virtuelle*), l'usager équipé d'un casque de visualisation stéréoscopique est laissé libre de mouvoir sa tête, voire de se déplacer à l'intérieur, dirait-on, d'un espace déclaré ‹virtuel›, lui-même construit selon les règles d'une ‹perspective› immédiatement déformable et transformable en fonction des mouvements de l'observateur et d'abord de la direction de son regard.

Que l'observateur puisse avoir la sensation d'explorer l'espace simulé qui s'ouvre (ou se déplie) devant lui ne suffit cependant pas à faire que son corps soit impliqué dans l'expérience autrement que sous des espèces strictement kinesthésiques, et qui n'admettent en définitive pas d'autre traduction qu'en termes de *position*. Ainsi en allait-il des «perspecteurs›d'Abraham Bosse, dont chacun allait déplaçant avec lui, nouée au point de l'œil, et l'orientant à son gré, sa propre pyramide visuelle. La différence étant que l'un est comme immergé dans un espace par principe instable, mais auquel il est strictement inféodé, quand bien même il réussirait à le contrôler parfaitement, là où les autres se mouvaient à leur gré dans l'espace déclaré ‹réel› mais dont ils ne connaissaient que sous l'espèce de vues fixes, d'images arrêtées, de virtualités suspendues. Quitte pour eux à tenter, comme s'y essaieront encore les photographes, d'y introduire le mouvement par le détour de figures elles-mêmes en suspens.

4. Comme on l'a maintes fois observé, et comme l'expérience du cinéma ou de la télévision le confirme à tout instant, le mouvement constitue en effet un facteur décisif en matière d'illusion: ce qu'on a nommé le *kinetic depth effect*, l'effet cinétique de profondeur est à même de jouer en l'absence de toute présentation stéréoscopique; et cela, que le mouvement prenne place et se déploie à l'intérieur de l'image, dans son cadre, quoi qu'il en soit de la position qu'occupe le *regardant*, ou que l'image soit appelée à se modifier en fonction des mouvements et des déplacements de l'observateur. Le spectateur est, au cinéma, d'autant mieux livré aux mouvements de la caméra qu'il est rivé à son siège, ainsi que l'est encore l'apprenti pilote dans un simulateur de vol, l'impact physique de la cascade d'images à laquelle il est exposé s'accroissant du fait que liberté lui est laissée de réagir par les mouvements appropriés: à cette différence près que des images de synthèse calculées en ‹temps réel› sont alors projetées sur une coupole hémisphérique au lieu qu'elles le sont, au cinéma, sur un écarn rectangulaire à deux dimensions, et dans le temps qui est celui du montage.

5. Différence de régime, donc, non pas tant du corps, que du *sujet*, dont la position est, ici comme là, loin d'aller de soi. Car c'est une chose pour le sujet d'avoir à se repérer comme tel, comme le voulait Lacan, dans le dispositif dénommé ‹tableau›, et c'en est une autre, pour lui, que d'ouvrir sa voie, de frayer son chemin dans un espace déclaré ‹virtuel›, mais qui n'en est pas moins astreint encore, jusqu'en ses transformations réglées, aux contraintes qui sont celles de la perspective. Si la production d'-images ‹virtuelles› suppose une manière de conversion par laquelle on passe d'un système de coordonnées qui aurait son origine dans l'oeil de l'observateur à un système de coordonnées qui correspondraient aux trois dimensions de l'espace dans lequel l'observateur est censé être plongé (suivant la donnée qui était déjà celle du cube perspectif), le principe en était acquis dès l'expérience inaugurale de Brunelleschi: celle-ci n'ayant eu en définitive pas d'autre objet que de montrer et de démontrer que le point dit de vue et le point dit de fuite se situaient sur une même ligne, perpendiculaire au plan du tableau, et qu'ils se trouvaient coïncider, par projection spéculaire, en ce lieu marqué d'un trou à travers lequel l'observateur était admis à contempler l'image au miroir d'un objet de peinture. A ceci près que la Renaissance aura su opérer und strict partage entre l'illusion et le trompe-l'œil, là où les opérations sur l'image qui ont cours en notre siècle nous portent au contraire à les confondre. A la feinte du trompe-l'œil, nul ne saurait se soustraire, quand bien même il en serait averti, pour autant qu'il se tienne au lieu qui lui est assigné. Ainsi en va-t-il, aujourd'hui, du spectateur au cinema (mais non de l'usager de la télévision, libre de ses déplacements comme l'est le visiteur au musée); ainsi en va-t-il du pilote dans un simulateur de vol; ainsi en va-t-il, dans une certaine mesure, du *regardant* équipé d'un casque de visualisation stéréoscopique qui lui laisse, sans doute, la possibilité de se mouvoir, mais pour mieux l'enclore, par le détour d'un écran lui-même virtuel, dans les rêts qui sont encore et toujours ceux de la perspective: l'illusion joue ici à plein, sans pour

autant qu'on soit en droit de parler de trompe-l'œil, au sens strict du terme.

6. Le débat portera en définitive sur le concept ou la notion de *projection*, et à travers elle sur la fonction qui peut être celle de l'*écran*. La projection que le paradigme perspectif nous porte à concevoir, par le détour de la peinture, aujourd'hui relayée par le cinéma, et d'une manière autrement sophistiquée par celui des images dites ‹virtuelles›, sous des espèces strictement optiques, là où la psychanalyse, pour ne parler que d'elle, en connaît sous l'espèce linguistique. La projection, aussi bien, qui peut en appeler à des effets d'écho, visuels autant que sonores, quand les déplacements du spectateur dans un espace celui-là ‹réel›, mais aménagé, programmé comme il convient, révèlent les virtualités d'une *partition* dont le dispositif perspectif aura dès l'abord proposé l'image paradigmatique sous l'espèce de la grille, du pavement quadrillé, de la scène en échiquier qui fait le sol de la représentation: l'écho supposant, pour l'heure, l'interposition d'un écran, fût-il celui d'un téléviseur, quand le sol n'en assume pas lui-même la fonction. Tout le problème étant de savoir de quelle incidence peut être, au registre phénoménologique, l'idée d'une projection numérique et d'un écran lui-même *virtuel*, celle-là même qu'imposent (et c'est là la véritable nouveauté) les images de synthèse et les techniques de simulation aujourd'hui à l'ordre du jour.

Hubert Damisch
Sechs Anmerkungen und einige Fragen zu einer Phänomenologie der sogenannten ‹virtuellen› Bilder

1. Es steht nun fest: wir haben bestimmt nicht mit der Perspektive abgeschlossen. Am wenigsten mit der Perspektive, die als diejenige der Maler angesehen wird, der *perspectiva artificialis*, der die traditionelle Optik der Antike und des Mittelalters zugerechnet wird, im Gegensatz zur *perspectiva naturalis*. Eben diese Perspektive, die auch die ‹wissenschaftliche› genannt wird und die im Quattrocento in dem Bereich auftauchte, der damals der der Malerei war, um sich bald als Paradigma par excellence des klassischen Darstellungssystems durchzusetzen und deren modernistische Version gewollt hat, daß ihre Zeit, ihr Schicksal, ihre historische Rolle mit Cézanne und dem Kubismus endete. Das Paradoxe dabei ist, daß über den Umweg der Photographie, des Kinos und von nun an auch der sogenannten synthetischen Bilder kein Zeitalter so massiv *informiert* gewesen sein wird, wie das unsere durch ein System, das ganz offensichtlich zu einer anderen Form von Geschichte als der strikt regionalen oder evolutionistischen gehörte: eine ‹vertikale› Geschichte, wie Merleau-Ponty sie nannte, die als solche die Möglichkeit einer Akkumulation und Sedimentierung in sich birgt ebenso wie die Geschichte der Philosophie

und der Wissenschaften, mit all den Auswirkungen von Vergraben, aber ebenso von Zutagetreten, von Verschieben, Neuordnen, Interferenz und Ineinanderstoßen, all die Möglichkeiten, die Gelegenheiten, die Vorgaben für die Ausgrabung, Exhumierung, der Erfindung sogar, die dieser Geschichte eine eigene archäologische Dimension verleihen. Die Perspektive – eine Angelegenheit der Vergangenheit? Tatsache ist, daß es gegenwärtig unmöglich ist, weiterhin von der Perspektive als ideologischer, verjährter und hinfälliger Schulung zu sprechen: das zugleich theoretische und praktische, begriffliche und handwerkliche, spekulative und nützliche Handwerkszeug, das sie in jedem Sinn des Wortes darstellt, dieses Handwerkszeug hat in der Tat im Bereich der synthetischen Bilder und Räume, der sogenannten ‹virtuellen› Environments, wieder Anerkennung gefunden. In ihrem Prinzip, ihrem Erzeugungsmodus, ihrem regulierten Funktionieren, bis hin zu den Erfahrungen, die sich für die Erfinder und Verwender ergeben, werden zwar die in diesem Bereich realisierten neuen Simulationstechniken zu einer tiefgreifenden Neuordnung des Darstellungssystems führen, aber dies ändert nichts an der Tatsache: das perspektivische Modell ist deswegen nicht weniger an der Arbeit, innerhalb von bestimmten Grenzen und in neuen Spielarten, die aber kontrastiv umso mehr seine Beständigkeit und seine Nützlichkeit beweisen. Zwar kann man daran arbeiten, die Perspektive aufzuheben, aber dennoch nur mit Mitteln, die zumindest teilweise ihre eigenen sind. Die Frage besteht nämlich darin, genau festzulegen, *inwieweit und bis zu welchem Punkt* das perspektivische Modell seine eigene Voruntersuchung einleitet, ihr eigenes Aufheben durchführt oder es zumindest reguliert.

2. Die Antwort, die man auf diese Frage geben kann, wird variieren, je nachdem ob man an einer strikt ideologischen Charakterisierung der *perspectiva artificialis* festhält, oder ob man in ihr ein Paradigma sieht, das man nicht einfach los wird, da es das klarste und kohärenteste Bild eines Darstellungssystems vor-

gibt und zugleich das effektivste Handwerkszeug darstellt. In welchem Bereich auch immer sie angewendet wird, die Simulationstechniken verwenden weniger Elemente aus der projektiven Geometrie als aus der Perspektive im althergebrachtesten Sinn des Wortes: und wie könnte es anders sein, da das Subjekt, oder wie wir sagen wollen, der Verwender, der Beobachter, derjenige, den man im klassischen Zeitalter den *Betrachter* nannte, dort prinzipiell einbezogen ist, und da, wenn es *Projektion* gibt und geben muß, sie nur dann Sinn macht, wenn sie sich einem bestimmten Punkt, wie dem Augenpunkt oder dem Subjekt *(il punto dell'occhio, dem Augenpunkt)* zuordnet und der, projektiv gesprochen, mit dem Fluchtpunkt in eins fällt, der das Bild des Augenpunktes auf der Projektionsfläche ist? Mit der Folge, daß die ersten Apparate, die dazu gedacht waren, dem Verwender perspektivische Bilder anzubieten, sich den Bewegungen seines Kopfes, ja seines Körpers entsprechend modifizieren und transformieren, ausdrücklich an das albertinische Modell gebunden sind: das Problem in diesem Stadium ist, ein solches System zu entwerfen, das sofort die Züge abschafft, die sich infolge einer Verschiebung oder einer Orientierungsveränderung des ‹Fensters› nicht mehr in den Rahmen, durch den die Aufführung zu sehen gegeben ist, einfügen können und das im Gegenteil alle die eintreten läßt, die vorher außerhalb des Blickfeldes blieben.

3. Wenn es einen Unterschied gibt zwischen einer perspektivischen Sicht, die auf der zweidimensionalen Fläche einer Wand oder eines Bildes aufgebaut ist, und einem künstlichen Raum der mit technischer Hilfe visualisierten Synthese von Bildern, würde er zunächst einem Unterschied des Funktionierens entsprechen: während die grundlegende Erfahrung, an die der Name Brunelleschi geknüpft ist, davon ausging, daß der Beobachter das Auge, und ein einziges, gegen die Rückseite einer mit einem Loch versehenen Tafel hält, auf die das Baptisterium von Florenz gemalt war, um es im Spiegel (die Perspektive ist also schon in ihrem Ursprung teilweise an das *virtuelle* Bild gebun-

den) zu betrachten, hat der mit einem Helm für stereoskopische Visualisierung ausgerüstete Verwender die Freiheit, seinen Kopf zu bewegen, ja sich ins Innere eines sogenannten ‹virtuellen› Raumes zu versetzen, der seinerseits nach den Regeln einer ‹Perspektive› konstruiert ist, die sofort entsprechend den Bewegungen des Beobachters und vor allem seiner Blickrichtung deformierbar und transformierbar ist. Daß der Beobachter die Empfindung haben kann, den simulierten Raum zu erforschen, der sich vor ihm öffnet (oder entfaltet), reicht unterdessen nicht dazu aus, seinen Körper anders in die Erfahrung einzubeziehen, als auf rein kinästhetische Weise, die definitiv keine andere Übersetzung als in Begriffen von *Position* zuläßt. So war es mit den ‹Wahrnehmern› Abraham Bosses, von denen jeder seine eigene, dem Augenpunkt verbundene und nach seinem Belieben orientierbare visuelle Pyramide zusammen mit sich selbst fortbewegte. Der Unterschied besteht darin, daß der eine in einem prinzipiell unbeständigen Raum wie untergetaucht ist, dem er aber strikt unterworfen ist, selbst wenn er es schaffen würde, ihn vollkommen zu kontrollieren; die anderen bewegten sich dagegen nach ihrem Belieben in dem sogenannten ‹realen› Raum, den sie aber nur durch unbewegliche Sicht, angehaltene Bilder, ausgesetzte Virtualitäten kennen. Ihnen bleibt die Möglichkeit, wie es die Photographen wieder versuchen, die Bewegung dort über den Umweg der ausgesetzten Figuren selber einzuführen.

4. Wie wir es viele Male beobachtet haben und wie die Kino- oder Fernseherfahrung es in jedem Augenblick bestätigt, ist die Bewegung tatsächlich ein entscheidender Faktor im Bereich der Illusion; das, was man den *kinetic depth effect* nennt, die kinetische Tiefenwirkung, ist imstande, in der Abwesenheit jeglicher stereoskopischer Präsentation zu funktionieren; und dies selbst wenn sich die Bewegung im Inneren des Bildes plaziert und entfaltet, in seinem Rahmen, unabhängig von der Position des Betrachters, oder wenn das Bild sich später den Bewegungen und dem Wechsel des Standorts des *Betrachters* entsprechend

verändert. Im Kino ist der Zuschauer umso stärker den Bewegungen der Kamera ausgeliefert, als er an seinen Sitz gekettet ist, ebenso wie der Fluganfänger in einem Flugsimulator, wobei der physische Einfluß der Bilderkaskade, der er ausgesetzt ist, aufgrund der Tatsache anwächst, daß er die Freiheit hat, mit angemessenen Bewegungen zu reagieren: mit dem Unterschied, daß in Echtzeit kalkulierte Synthesebilder dann auf eine hemisphärische Kuppel projiziert werden, anstatt in der Montagezeit auf einen zweidimensionalen, rechteckigen Bildschirm wie im Kino.

5. Unterschied im Funktionieren also, nicht so sehr des Körpers als vielmehr des Subjekts, dessen Position hier wie dort weit davon entfernt ist, selbstverständlich zu sein. Denn es ist eine Sache für das Subjekt, wie Lacan es wollte, sich im System ‹Bild› als solches zu orten und eine andere, einen Pfad einzuschlagen, sich einen Weg zu bahnen im sogenannten ‹virtuellen› Raum, der aber den Zwängen der Perspektive unterworfen ist bis hinein in seine geregelten Transformationen. Wenn die Produktion ‹virtueller› Bilder eine Art und Weise der Umkehrung voraussetzt, von der aus man von einem Koordinatensystem, das seinen Ursprung im Auge des Betrachters hätte, zu einem Koordinatensystem übergeht, das mit den drei Dimensionen des Raumes übereinstimmen würde, von dem angenommen wird, daß der Betrachter in ihn eintaucht, (der Gegebenheit folgend, die schon die des perspektivischen Kubus war), war das Prinzip bereits mit der grundlegenden Erfahrung Brunelleschis da: diese hatte nämlich letztendlich keinen anderen Gegenstand, als zu zeigen und zu beweisen, daß der sogenannte Augenpunkt und der sogenannte Fluchtpunkt auf einer Linie liegen, senkrecht zur Fläche des Bildes und daß sie, wenn sie durch Spiegelprojektion zusammenfallen, dann eben an dem durch das Loch gekennzeichneten Ort, durch das der *Beobachter* das Spiegelbild eines gemalten Gegenstands betrachten durfte. Mit dem Unterschied, daß die Renaissance Illusion und Trompe-l'oeil streng zu trennen wußte, während die Bildbe-

handlungen, die in unserem Jahrhundert geläufig sind, uns im Gegenteil dahin führen, sie zu verwechseln. Kein Mensch kann sich den Verstellungen des Trompe-l'oeil entziehen, selbst wenn er darüber im Bilde wäre, falls er sich an den vorbestimmten Ort hält. So geht es heute einem Zuschauer im Kino (aber nicht dem Fernsehzuschauer, der sich so frei bewegt wie der Museumsbesucher); ebenso geht es dem Piloten im Flugsimulator; ebenso, bis zu einem gewissen Grad, dem mit einem Helm für stereoskopische Visualisierung ausgestatteten Betrachter, der ihm wohl die Möglichkeit läßt, sich zu bewegen, der ihn aber umso mehr über den Umweg eines Bildschirms, der selber virtuell ist, in Netzen einfängt, die immer noch die der Perspektive sind: die Illusion funktioniert hier vollständig, ohne daß man von Trompe-l'oeil im engen Sinne des Worts sprechen könnte.

6. Die Diskussion wird schließlich den Entwurf oder die Auffassung der *Projektion* zum Gegenstand haben und führt über sie zur Funktion des *Bildschirms*. Die Projektion, die das perspektivische Paradigma uns über den Umweg der Malerei, heute abgelöst vom Kino und auf kompliziertere Weise durch die sogenannten ‹virtuellen› Bilder begreiflich macht, ist unter rein optischen Aspekten zu sehen, während die Psychoanalyse, um nur von ihr zu sprechen, die Projektion auch unter linguistischen Aspekten kennt. Die Projektion, die ebenso visuelle wie klangliche Echoeffekte verwendet, wenn der Standortwechsel des Zuschauers diesmal im ‹realen›, aber eingerichteten, entsprechend programmierten Raum erfolgt, die Virtualitäten einer Partitur enthüllen, deren perspektivisches System schon beim ersten Anblick das paradigmatische Bild als Raster, als karierte Fläche, als Schachbrettmuster, das den Grund der Darstellung bildet: das Echo setzt nämlich heutzutage das Dazwischenschieben eines Bildschirms, selbst eines Fernsehbildschirms an, wenn der Grund selbst die Funktion des Bildschirms nicht übernimmt. Das ganze Problem besteht darin, zu wissen, welche Bedeutung, phänomenologisch gesprochen, die Idee einer numerischen Projektion und eines Bildschirms

haben kann, der selber *virtuell* ist; gerade diese Projektion, die uns (und darin besteht die wirkliche Neuerung) die Synthesebilder und die Simulationstechniken aufzwingen, die heute an der Tagesordnung sind.

Aus dem Französischen übersetzt von Antje Quast

Hubert Damisch
Six Notes and Some Queries Concerning a Phenomenology of So-Called ‹Virtual› Images

1. One thing has been ascertained by now: we have definitely not done with perspective yet, at least with what is considered to be the painter's *perspectiva artificialis*, as opposed to the *perspectiva naturalis*, whence resumes traditional optics, both classical and medieval. It is the very same perspective we still define as ‹scientific› and which made its appearance in the Italian Quattrocento, at the time, incidentally, in the field of painting, from where it was soon to impose itself as the exemplary paradigm of classical representation, and with whose tradition, fortune, and historic importance the modernist Vulgate has attempted to bring to an end in Cézanne and Cubism. The paradox, though, being that through the evasive influence of photography, the cinema, and these days so-called synthetic imagery, no other period in history has been so massively *informed* as our own; an apparatus which relieves us of any evidence from history other than a strictly regional and evolutionary one: a ‹vertical› history, as Merleau-Ponty called it, which is open to accumulation and sedimentation with all their cover-up effects, as well as entailing levelling-out, displacement, modification, interference, magnification, and all the other possibilities, opportunities, and

propositions of search, excavation, and exhumation, indeed invention, to the largest extent ever possible in the history of the natural sciences or of philosophy, and which really confers an archaeological dimension on this type of history.

Perspective, a thing of the past? Right now it is actually impossible to talk about much longer as an out-of-date, ideological frame of reference fallen from grace: the entire theoretical and practical, conceptual and instrumental, speculative and utilitarian device it represents in all senses of the word, this device has in effect regained its freedom of the city built on the land of synthetic images and spaces, of environments labelled ‹virtual›. But as to their underlying principle, their implementation, adjustable function, and right through to the experiences they engender both for the part of the inventor as much as for the user, what the techniques of simulation at work in that land finally amount to is a serious modification of the representational apparatus which changes basically nothing about the state of affairs that the perspective model is still no less at work, of course within precise limits and under new conditions which could, however, not serve any better to illustrate its continued pertinence and usefulness. No doubt you could further its ‹demise›, but only by means that are at least in part its very own. The question then arising is how to determine in precisely what way and *just how far* the perspective model will inherently institute its own proceedings against itself, implement its own demise, or at the very least perhaps control that process?

2. The answer you will be tempted to give will vary according to whether you tend towards a strictly ideological definition of *perspectiva artificialis* or whether you acknowledge it to be a paradigm of which you cannot avail yourself so readily, in that it still propounds the clearest and most coherent conception of what the representational apparatus might be, at the same time as providing its most efficient tool. Whatever their application, the techniques of simulation borrow less from geometric projection than from perspective in the most conventional sense of

the term: moreover, where does it leave us, seeing that it implies that the subject, or user as we should say now, the observer who used to be called *beholder* in classical times, is fundamentally involved; and if there is, or indeed has to be, *projection*, then it has only one purpose, which is to arrange itself around a point such as predetermined by the eye or the subject which would, projectionally speaking, in fact converge on what is known as the vanishing point which generates the former's image on the projection plane. One consequence seems to be that the first devices developed to provide the user with a perspective image that could be modified and transformed as a function of respective head or even body movements were to have explicitly renounced the Alberti model. The problem at this stage is to conceive of an apparatus whose traits are such that they are being eliminated instantly in accordance with a movement or directional change of the ‹window›, can no longer be retrieved for reinscription in the setting across which the spectacle should just have unfolded before your eyes, and which instead now push all the impressions that were before lying outside the field of vision into that setting.

3. If indeed there should be a difference between a perspective view constructed on the two-dimensional plane of a wall or painting and an artificial space visualized by means of image-synthesizing techniques, then it would primarily correspond to a difference of operation. Whereas the basic experience with which we associate Brunelleschi's name was inferring the observer place an eye, and one eye only, on a hole through the back of a panel painted with a view of the Florence Baptistry to look on its image projected in sharp perspective in a facing mirror (the discovery of the rules of perspective thus being in part linked to a *virtual* image), the user equipped with a stereoscopic data visor is free to move his head, or even move around completely, ‹within› as we say, something known as a ‹virtual› space, itself laid out in compliance with the rules of a ‹perspective› that may be instantly deformed or transformed as a function of

the observer's movement or initially a change in the direction of his glance.

That the observer is able to have a sensation of exploring a space which opens up (or collapses) right in front of him does not suffice for his entire body to be involved in the experience as well, in any other way than under conditions that are strictly cinesthetic and which cannot be translated on any basis other than a stationary one. Thus each one of Abraham Busse's ‹prospectors›, tied down by the limited scope of his point of view which he is free to cast in any direction he wishes, was taking around with him his very own visual pyramid. The difference is that the former is as if immersed in some space that is basically transmutable but to which he is strictly subservient, no matter how perfectly he would succeed in controlling it, whereas the latter can comport themselves freely in a space perceived as ‹real›, but with which they can only familiarize themselves by a series of fixed views focussed on momentary images, suspended virtualities. They may well attempt to introduce movement by turning around shapes which are themselves in abeyance, something photographers are still vainly trying to do now.

4. As we have seen time and again, and as has been continually confirmed by experience in the cinema or with television, movement in effect constitutes a decisive illusory factor: what is known as the *kinetic depth effect* is enacted without any need for stereoscopic presentation and quite regardless of whether it takes place and is deployed within the framework of an image that depends on the stationary position of a *spectator* or whether it may be changed at will by the movements of an observer. In the cinema the spectator is subjected that much more effectively to the movement of the camera if he is quite firmly tied to his seat; similarly the trainee pilot is tied to the seat of his flight simulator, only that the physical impact of the torrent of images he is subjected to may increase or decrease depending on the fact that he is left with the freedom to react with corresponding

movements. The only slight difference is that the calculated synthetic images are projected in ‹real time› on a hemispheric dome instead of a two-dimensional screen in the time of the montage.

5. The different conditions would thus denote not so much the body, but rather the subject whose position in both cases is quite removed from itself. For it is one thing for the subject to have to physically repair, as observed by Lacan, to the location of the device called ‹picture›, and quite another to open its eyes and burst through some ‹virtual› space whose regulated transformations are nonetheless still subject to the constraints that belong to the rules of perspective. If you adapt to the generation of ‹virtual› images by converting a system of co-ordinates that originated in the eye of the beholder into a system of co-ordinates that corresponds to the three dimensions of a space into which the observer has the sensation of having been plunged (within the limits set by the perspective cube), whose principles derive from the inaugurational experiments by Brunelleschi, whose sole aim had been to demonstrate that the point of view and the vanishing point both converged on the same perpendicular line on the planar painting, and that they would coincidentally fall via specular projection onto a point marked by a hole through which the spectator was looking at the mirror-image of a painted object. As precisely as the Renaissance was able to distinguish between illusion and trompe l'oeil, so the kind of operations being performed on the image these days are instead threatening to confound that distinction. Nothing can elude the sham of trompe l'oeil anymore, no matter how you might try to avoid that fate, or how firmly something might seem to occupy an assigned place. Today this applies just as much to the cinema spectator (but not the television viewer who may move around as freely as the visitor to the museum); it would apply to the pilot in his flight simulator, and to some extent to the *onlooker equipped* with a stereoscopic visor which naturally allows him to move, but only in order to

be engulfed all the more with the detours afforded by a screen that is itself only virtual, trapping him in a web of rules which are still those of perspective. Here, illusion is as strong as ever, without us even speaking of trompe l'oeil in the strictest sense of the word.

6. This discussion inevitably leads us to the concept or notion of *projection* and hence what the function of the *screen* could be. Projection which the perspective paradigm has led us to conceive via a detour in painting , and which is today relayed by the cinema in a manner that is sophisticated, but different to the kind of projection generated by ‹virtual› images; projection in strictly optical terms, as opposed to what psychoanalysis is talking about in linguistic terms. Projection which might provoke effects that echo, both visually and aurally, the comportment of the spectator in ‹real› space; however, adapted and programmed for convenience they reveal the virtualities of a *division* whose perspective framework, right from the start, will have provided for a paradigmatic image under a grid system, the chequered grid on which the draughtsman will lay out his design for representation: For the time being that echo is based on the interpositioning of a screen or televisor, whilst the plane of the canvas alone cannot assume that function. The problem now is to know what the repercussions would be on a phenomenological level of the idea of digitalized projection, and a screen that would itself also be *virtual*. This is the question (and real novelty) behind synthetic images and the simulation techniques that are the order of the day today.

Translated from the French original by J. von Stein

Paul Virilio
La grande optique

«Plus les télescopes seront perfectionnés et plus il y aura d'étoiles.» *(Gustave Flaubert)*

Je voudrais vous parler du dédoublement de la vue et de l'émergence d'une seconde optique: celle qui rend possible aujourd'hui la TELECONFERENCE entre Tokyo et Paris.
Certains ont parlé à ce propos, il y a déjà quelques années, d'un TROU DANS L'ESPACE, d'autres plus récemment, d'un TROU DANS LE TEMPS, le temps réel de la transmission instantanée d'événements historiques, en particulier de la guerre du Golfe. Cette hésitation sémantique me semble caractéristique du trouble de la perception qui affecte désormais nos sociétés devant le progrès des télé-technologies et le déclin de l'importance de l'optique géométrique, OPTIQUE PASSIVE de l'espace de la matière (du verre, de l'eau ou de l'air) et qui ne rend compte finalement, que de la proximité immédiate de l'homme.
Si vous le voulez bien, nous intitulerons cette dernière *la petite optique* pour réserver à l'optique ondulatoire, OPTIQUE ACTIVE du temps de la vitesse de la lumière, le titre de *grande optique*, puisque celle-ci passe outre à la notion classique d'*horizon*.
Il est évident aussi, que l'électro-optique des ondes véhiculant le signal VIDEO introduit en fait à la question de la digitalisation de ce signal, dont chacun s'accorde à reconnaître l'importance, non seulement dans le domaine de l'observation astronomique, avec les prouesses de l'optique dite ‹adaptative›, mais surtout, dans la mise en œuvre récente des *espaces de la réalité* virtuelle.

Puisque l'OPTIQUE est la partie de la physique qui traite des propriétés de la lumière et donc des phénomènes de la visualisation, au dédoublement de la vue s'ajoute aussi le dédoublement de la lumière elle-même, non seulement comme jadis, entre lumière NATURELLE (le soleil) et ARTIFICIELLE (l'électricité) mais encore, entre lumière DIRECTE (soleil et électricité) et lumière INDIRECTE (la vidéosurveillance) qui résulte de l'interaction en temps réel des phénomènes optiques et de l'électronique, d'où le terme d'OPTO.ELECTRONIQUE.
Tout ceci nous amène à parler maintenant, non plus uniquement, comme les philosophes de l'âge classique, de *l'étendue* et de la *durée* de l'espace de la matière, mais encore de *l'épaisseur optique* du temps de la lumière et de son amplification ‹opto-électronique›qui nécessitent le deplassement de la perspective géométrique de la Renaissance italienne, par une perspective électronique: celle du temps réel de l'émission et de la réception instantanée des signaux audio-vidéo.
Ainsi, devant le récent renouvellement de l'optique *géométrique* des rayons lumineux par l'optique *ondulatoire* du rayonnement ‹électro-magnétique› des particules qui véhiculent la vision et l'audition, nous assistons à l'émergence d'un dernier type de transparence: *la transparence des apparences instantanément transmises à distance*, TRANS.APPARENCE qui vient dès lors compléter (pour ainsi dire, parachever) celle, naturelle, de l'atmosphère terrestre, occasionnant du même coup, une sorte de redoublement ‹stéréoscopique› des apparences sensibles, de la représentation du Monde et donc, indirectement, de l'esthétique elle-même.
A l'esthétique de l'apparition des objets ou des personnes se détachant sur *l'horizon apparant* de l'unité de temps et de lieu de la perspective classique s'adjoint l'esthétique de la disparition de personnages lointains surgissant sur l'absence d'horizon d'un écran cathodique où l'unité de temps l'emporte sur celle du lieu de la rencontre: *la perspective du temps réel* de la grande optique supplantant définitivement les performances de la petite opti-

que de *la perspective de l'espace réel*, le point de fuite de la focalisation des rayons lumineux cédant soudain la primauté à la fuite de tous les points (les pixels) de l'image télévisée.
Dès lors, la transparence *directe* de l'espace qui permet à chacun d'entre nous d'apercevoir ses voisins immédiats, se complète de la transparence *indirecte* du temps de la vitesse des ondes électro-magnétiques qui transmettent nos images, notre voix et demain, n'en doutons pas, notre ACTION réciproque, grâce au costume de données (DATA.SUIT) qui permettra non seulement la télé.vision ou la télé.audition, mais encore la TELE.ACTION en commun.
Mais avant d'aborder le cadre de la future TELE.EXISTENCE, revenons si vous le voulez bien, sur cette GRANDE OPTIQUE électromagnétique qui permet aujourd'hui de *nous réunir à distance,* aux antipodes de la planète.
A l'élairage *direct* de l'astre solaire qui décompose en journées distinctes l'activité de nos années, s'ajoute désormais pour nous l'éclairage *indirect*, la ‹lumière› d'une technologie qui favorise une sorte de dédoublement de la personnalité du temps entre: le temps réel de nos *activités immédiates,* où nous agissons à la fois ici *et* maintenant et le temps réel d'une *interactivité médiatique* qui privilégie le ‹maintenant› du créneau horaire de l'émission télévisée, au détriment de ‹l'ici›, c'est-à-dire de l'espace du lieu de recontre.
Comment vivre vraiment si *ici* n'est plus et si tout est *maintenant?* Comment survivre demain au télescopage instantané d'une réalité devenue ubiquitaire se décomposant en deux temps aussi réels l'un que l'autre: celui de la *présence* ici et maintenant, et celui d'une *télé-présence* à distance, par delà l'horizon des apparences sensibles?
Comment gérer rationnellement le dédoublement, non seulement entre REALITES VIRTUELLE et ACTUELLE, mais encore entre l'horizon *apparent* qui balise la limite de perception de mon activité coutumière et l'horizon *trans-apparent* d'un écran qui entr'ouvre soudain une sorte de fenêtre temporelle pour interagir ailleurs et souvent très loin?

A moins de nier, à l'instar de Marvin Minsky, l'importance de l'optique ‹analogique› et donc, de l'horizon des apparences, il nous faut désormais impérativement interroger le caractère STEREOSCOPIQUE, non seulement du ‹relief des apparences› et de la troisième dimension spatiale, mais surtout la quatrième, le *relief temporel* occasionné cette fois par le dédoublement entre les proximités spatiale et temporelle, le relief d'un monde désormais surexposé à l'amplification électro-optique de sa profondeur de champ.

‹*La présence n'est présence qu'à distance, et cette distance est absolue, c'est-à-dire irréductible*›, écrivait Maurice Blanchot ... Aujourd'hui, où la notion de ‹distance› a cédé la place en physique, à celle d'une ‹puissance› d'émission instantanée, l'optique ondulatoire aboutit à une ‹fluctuation des apparences› où la distance n'est plus, comme le souhaitait le poète, la profondeur de la présence, mais seulement son intermittence. L'intervalle d'*espace* (signe négatif) et l'intervalle de *temps* (signe positif) ayant depuis peu cédé leur primauté à l'intervalle de signe nul de *la vitesse-lumière* des ondes véhiculant l'information, venons-en maintenant aux problèmes posés par l'innovation d'une ‹digitalisation des signaux› (audio-vidéo et tactile) permettant non plus comme naguère avec l'esthétique de l'apparition, la mise en œuvre de la REPRESENTATION de la réalité sensible mais bel et bien sa PRESENTATION intempestive grâce aux capteurs, aux senseurs et autres ‹télédétecteurs› de ce que l'on nomme TELEPRESENCE.

Rappelons au passage, qu'il n'y a de véritable présence au Monde – au Monde propre de l'expérience sensible – que par le truchement de l'égo-centration d'un *présent-vivant*, autrement dit, par l'existence d'un corps propre vivant *ici et maintenant*.

La question posée par l'intermittente ‹télé-présence-à-distance› introduit donc, n'en déplaise aux cognitivistes, une série d'interrogations analogues à celles posées, en physiques, par la fameuse DISTANCE de PLANCK: lorsque l'extrême éloignement spa-

tial cède soudain la place à l'extrême proximité du temps réel des échanges, *demeure cependant un écart irréductible*.
Malgré l'absence d'intervalle due à l'inexistence de l'espace réel de la rencontre, l'interface de signe nul des ondes électromagnétiques permettant la TELECOMMUNICATION, interdit la confusion habituelle de ‹l'ici et maintenant›, l'instantanéité de l'interactivité n'éliminant jamais la distinction entre l'acte et l'agir à distance.
Il en est de même d'ailleurs, dans le cas d'une TELE.EXISTENCE en commun, et ceci quel que soit le degré de proximité des téléacteurs réunis à distance.
Ainsi, à côté de l'utilisation du casque (VPL) et du costume de données (DATA.SUIT) dans le domaine de l'espace virtuel (CYBERSPACE) qui provoque un premier dédoublement de la personnalité du temps entre ACTUEL et VIRTUEL, il existe aussi une autre pratique de ce type d'équipement *électro-ergonomique* qui concerne, cette fois, l'espace actuel des échanges à distance: celle du TELEOPERATEUR (ou, si l'on préfère, du télémanipulateur) grâce aux progrès récents de la TELE.TACTILITE, où le ‹haut-relief› du toucher à distance vient compléter la ‹haute-fidélité› sonore et la ‹haute-définition› visuelle.
D'où l'émergence prochaine d'un volume purement ‹temporel› et donc, *la venue d'une perspective du toucher en temps réel* qui viendra bouleverser celle de la visualisation classique des perspectivistes du Quattrocento et donc la vision du Monde du siècle prochain.
On remarquera en effet que *la grande optique ondulatoire* ne s'attache plus seulement à la portée visuelle mais qu'elle entraîne aussi l'intégralité de la perception des apparences sensibles, y compris le sens du toucher, et ceci: *parce que le temps, le temps réel du troisième intervalle du genre lumière des ondes électromagnétiques,* l'emporte définitivement sur l'espace réel de la matière, sur ‹l'étendue›, la ‹durée› des substances composant l'étroit environnement humain.
Grâce aujourd'hui aux techniques dites de ‹retour d'effort›, au

feed-back du gant de données TELETACT récemment commercialisé, et demain, à la combinaison télétactile intégrale où le toucher, l'impact, sera celui du corps entier, nous assisterons à la production industrielle d'un dédoublement de la personnalité, non pas au clonage de l'homme vivant, mais à la création technique de l'un des plus anciens mythes: celle du DOUBLE, d'un double ‹électro-ergonomique› à la présence spectrale, autre dénomination du fantôme ou du mort-vivant.

Impossible, en effet, de ne pas évoquer la dramaturgie propre à ce genre de technologies nouvelles.

Le traumatisme de la naissance n'atteignant pas seulement l'enfant, le sujet, mais aussi l'objet, l'instrument qui émerge, il nous faut tenter de découvrir ‹l'accident originel› spécifique à ce genre d'innovation technique.

A moins d'oublier volontairement *l'invention du naufrage* dans celle du navire ou de l'accident ferroviaire dans l'apparition du train, il nous faut interroger la face cachée des technologies nouvelles, avant que cette dernière ne s'impose malgré nous à l'évidence.

Déjà, la *contamination virale* apporte une première réponse à la question de la négativité des circuits électroniques, mais permettez-moi de vous indiquer une autre piste de recherche: celle de la *pollution écologique*.

Pollution, non seulement des ‹substances› atmosphériques, hydrosphériques ou autres, mais encore de celle inaperçue des ‹distances›, cette pollution DROMOSPHERIQUE des distances de temps qui réduit à rien ou presque, l'étendue d'une étroite planète suspendue dans le vide sidéral.

Après la prise en compte, combien légitime pour nous autres terriens, de la pollution de LA NATURE, ne conviendrait-il pas de nous attacher à étudier aussi, cette POLLUTION DE LA GRANDEUR NATURE, occasionnée par l'essor des technologies du temps réel?

Alors que la PETITE OPTIQUE géométrique permettait de percevoir, et donc de concevoir le monde propre comme

‹étendue› et ‹durée› c'est-à-dire comme *grandeur géographique*, grâce à la vastitude même de l'espace réel des apparences, inversement la GRANDE OPTIQUE ondulatoire dissout aujourd'hui l'ampleur du milieu humain.
La puissance d'émission et de réception en temps réel des différents signaux aliénant la nature des distances de temps, l'optique active des ondes électromagnétiques *exploite* la profondeur de champ, la réalité même du monde propre, au point de la réduire à rien, ou presque, aboutissant par là, à un sentiment catastrophique d'incarcération pour une humanité littéralement privée d'horizon ...
En effet, là où la petite optique *passive* de l'espace de la matière – de l'air de l'eau, du verre des lentilles – se contentait de donner à contempler le GRAND MONDE des apparences, la grande optique *active* du temps de la vitesse de la lumière débouche (par-delà tout horizon) sur la perception intermittente du PETIT MONDE de la transparence des ondes supportant les divers signaux: ‹transapparence› qui élimine la limite habituelle de la ligne d'horizon au profit du seul cadre de l'écran; ‹horizon au carré› d'une sorte de réalité perspective dédoublée; STEREO.REALITE. où les ‹graves› et les ‹aigus› du relief sonore de la haute fidélité acoustique seraient remplacés d'une part, par la gravité, la pesanteur des corps et donc des distances réelles d'un monde *entier* et d'autre part, par l'absence de poids, de gravité, des signaux d'une sorte de haute-définition visuelle et tactile, s'inscrivant dans le domaine exotique des champs électromagnétiques.
La grandeur-nature des *distances physiques* ayant ainsi subi la loi de la *puissance microphysique* des ondes transmettant l'audition, la vision et demain le toucher (le tact-à-distance), comment ne pas évoquer le risque pour l'humanité d'une perte du monde propre? Et donc, comment ne pas redouter dès maintenant, la venue d'un profond sentiment d'enfermement pour l'homme, dans un environnement à la fois privé d'horizon et *d'épaisseur optique?*

A Edgar Degas, à qui l'on citait la phrase romantique d'Amiel, ‹*Un paysage c'est un état d'âme*›, le peintre français rétorqua, ‹*Non, c'est un état d'yeux!*›
Aujourd'hui, préoccupés par l'équilibre d'un milieu humain gravement menacé par les déjections industrielles, ne conviendrait-il pas d'ajouter aux soucis de l'ECOLOGIE VERTE, ceux d'une ECOLOGIE GRISE qui s'intéresserait à la dégradation post-industrielle de la profondeur de champ du paysage terrestre?

Lancée il y a 20 ans, le 2 Mars 1972, la sonde spatiale PIONEER 10 est le premier objet fabriqué de main d'homme à quitter le système solaire, mais c'est aussi et peut-être surtout, *une sorte d'étalon des différentes grandeurs cosmiques.*
Situé quelque part, à *8 milliards de kilomètres de la terre,* l'engin américain émet chaque jour des signaux qui mettent *7 heures trente* pour atteindre les antennes de la NASA. Le télescope et l'ensemble des instruments embarqués à bord de la sonde demeurant opérationnel, le ‹temps réel› des messages transmis par PIONEER équivaut donc pratiquement au décallage horaire entre TOKYO et PARIS ...
Véritable capteur électronique de l'ampleur de l'univers, la sonde spatiale nous renseigne ainsi en permanence et en un feed-back quel que peu différé, sur la restriction progressive de l'étendue terrestre.
En effet, si comme l'écrit Gustave Flaubert, ‹Plus les télescopes seront perfectionnés et plus il y aura d'étoiles›, il omet encore les retombées de cette soudaine dilatation optique: *plus la perception de l'outre-monde sera développée et moins il y aura de monde, de terre entière.*
Plus les moyens de connaître par-delà l'horizon seront perfectionnés et plus l'étendue terrestre, la ‹durée› du monde de l'expérience sensible seront abaissées, réduites à rien, à moins que rien, c'est ce qu'on appelle vulgairement: *l'autre bout de la lorgnette!*
Remarquons-le au passage, si la petite optique géométrique

s'était naguère illustrée avec Galilée, en révélant à nouveau aux hommes que la TERRE TOURNE, la grande optique électronique s'attache quant à elle, à révéler que L'UNIVERS SE DILATE ... deux ‹temps›, deux époques de la perception et deux ‹mouvements› radicalement différents.

Mais revenons à notre sonde spatiale destinée à observer de près les astres du système solaire, en particulier JUPITER. Propulsé par la force de gravitation de cette planète, l'engin américain poursuit inexorablement sa course vers l'infini, *à la vitesse de 46.000 kilomètres à l'heure*. Mais de quelle HEURE et de quel KILOMETRE s'agit-il puisque la sonde automatique n'est en fait *nulle part*, au point que les hommes qui ont assuré son lancement et sont aujourd'hui à la retraite, tel B.J. O'Brian, déclarent: ‹C'est impressionnant, *c'est même à devenir fou!*›

Malgré l'aspect rationnel, scientifique, de cette loi de *l'expansion universelle* inaugurée il y a bientôt soixante ans par Edwin Hubble et quelques autres, nul n'apprécie vraiment les effets de ce mouvement sur la perception coutumière, sur l'expérience immédiate, alors qu'un grand phénomène d'attraction, de succion, absorbe aujourd'hui l'effet de réel des apparences terrestres.

Préoccupé par la fuite de la fameuse ‹couche d'ozone›, aucun d'entre nous ne perçoit encore cette progressive déréalisation de l'horizon terrestre, cette autre ‹fuite› qui résulte de la primauté prochaine de la PERSPECTIVE DU TEMPS REEL de l'optique ondulatoire sur celle de l'espace réel de l'optique géométrique du QUATTROCENTO. ‹BIG.VIEW› qui vient pourtant logiquement parachever le célèbre BIG.BANG de l'astrophysique contemporaine.

On peut même légitimement se demander aujourd'hui si Edwin Hubble, l'un des pères-fondateurs du *principe de la dilatation cosmique* (grâce notamment, aux performances du télescope du Mont Wilson) n'a pas été en 1929, la première victime de l'illusion d'optique annoncée par Flaubert, comme semblait d'ailleurs le soupçonner Albert Einstein à l'époque ... Quant aux récents apôtres du BIG.BANG, ils pourraient bien eux aussi, être les victimes du décor d'une transparence astronomique accrue par la vitesse de transmission des signaux des télescopes ou des radiotélescopes.

Grandissement, rapetissement optiques, effet doppler de décalage vers le rouge du spectre des galaxies, autres dénominations de l'accélération et de la décélération des apparences où la DROMOSCOPIE – lumière de la vitesse – *éclaire littéralement la réalité perceptible*, une réalité dont le RELIEF STEREOSCOPIQUE provoque déjà nombre de troubles de la perception dont il faudrait, je crois, finir par tenir compte, puisque la notion même de ‹proximité physique› risque de s'en trouver bientôt radicalement changée. La GRANDE OPTIQUE qui permet de tester l'éloignement astrophysique le plus vaste, contribuant aussi mais inversement, à invalider la proximité physique la plus voisine.

Observons, en guise de confirmation de ce propos, qu'il y a vingt ans, avant d'assister au lancement de la sonde spatiale PIONEER, les responsables jugèrent bon d'apposer sur l'engin une plaque d'identité, outre la figuration du système solaire avec la planète Terre et les silhouettes d'un homme et d'une femme, les américains ajoutèrent, pour donner une idée de nos dimensions à d'éventuels extra-terrestres, un atome d'hydrogène: *la distance entre le noyau et son unique électron définissant l'unité de mesure*.

Alors même que la sonde qui allait être lancée, était destinée à tester la démesure de la dilatation cosmique, les scientifiques redonnaient ainsi à la notion de ‹distance minimale› sa fonction d'évaluation de cette GRANDEUR NATURE qui est bel et bien, notre habitat premier.

Qu'on le veuille ou non, il y a maintenant pour chacun de nous, dédoublement de la représentation du Monde et donc de sa REALITE. Dédoublement entre activité et interactivité, présence et téléprésence, existence et téléexistence.

Confrontés au caractère STEREOSCOPIQUE d'un réel partagé entre optique et électro-optique, acoustique et électro-acoustique, tact et télé-tactilité, nous sommes mis en demeure d'abandonner nos coutumes de voir et de penser, pour appréhender un nouveau type de ‹relief› qui remet en question jusqu'à l'utilité pratique de la notion d'HORIZON et donc, la ‹perspective› qui nous permettait jusqu'à présent de nous reconnaître *ici et maintenant*.

Tout cela, parce que l'unique source de ‹lumière› et donc de ‹réalité› de jadis, s'est elle-même dédoublée, l'ombre (directe) des rayons du soleil ou de la lampe électrique se complétant maintenant des ‹zones d'ombre› (indirectes) de l'absence d'émission des signaux électroniques, la TELESURVEILLANCE venant soudain supplanter l'éclairage des choses, la perception de VISU de l'observateur habituel.

Première génération de l'histoire à assister à la conquête de l'espace mais surtout à celle d'une vitesse qui permet la conquête du temps réel de l'instantanéité, nous assistons également à la révélation d'une dernière forme d'énergie: l'ENERGIE CINEMATIQUE, énergie ‹en images› où si l'on préfère ‹en informations›, qui vient ainsi s'ajouter aux énergies potentielle et cinétique.

Troisième forme énergétique qui permet, non plus uniquement, la GEOMETRISATION de la vision du monde, à l'instar de celle des perspectivistes de la Renaissance italienne, mais bien son INDUSTRIALISATION, l'artisanat des apparences élaboré par les tenants de l'optique ‹passive› de l'espace de la matière cèdant la place à l'industrie de l'optique ‹active› (électro-optique) du temps de la lumière.

En effet, lorsque le relativiste contemporain de l'ère einsteinienne, remplace la notion de ‹distance› physique par celle d'une ‹puissance› d'émission et de réception microphysique instantanée, annulant du même coup l'ancienne primauté de la conception perspectiviste de l'ère galiléenne – ajoutant même un troisième intervalle du genre ‹lumière› aux intervalles classiques du genre ‹espace› et du genre ‹temps› – il provoque une mutation du principe de réalité où le caractère AUTOMATI-

QUE des représentations équivaut à une normalisation de la perception, permise par l'utilisation de l'énergie de synthèse de l'imagerie électronique et ceci, dans le domaine des représentations ‹analogiques› aussi bien que ‹numériques›.
Nous remarquerons pour finir, que la TELEPRESENCE en perspective et donc la TELE.EXISTENCE en commun, par-delà les limites de proximité habituelles, n'élimine pas seulement la ‹ligne› de l'horizon apparent au profit de l'absence de ligne d'un horizon profond et imaginaire, mais qu'elle remet en cause la notion même de RELIEF, le toucher, la TACTILITE A DISTANCE venant gravement perturber, non seulement la distinction entre ‹actuel› et ‹virtuel› comme l'expliquent aujourd'hui les adeptes du CYBERSPACE, mais la réalité même du PROCHE et du LOINTAIN, remettant ainsi en question, notre présence *ici et maintenant* et découplant de ce fait, les conditions de nécessité de l'expérience sensible.

Paul Virilio
Die große Optik

«Je besser die Teleskope werden, desto mehr Sterne wird es geben». *(Gustave Flaubert)*

Ich möchte gern über die Aufspaltung des Sehens und das Auftauchen einer zweiten Optik sprechen, einer Optik, die heute die TELEKONFERENZ zwischen Tokio und Paris möglich macht. In dieser Angelegenheit haben gewisse Personen schon vor einigen Jahren von einem RAUMLOCH gesprochen, andere vor kurzem von einem ZEITLOCH, der Echtzeit der Direktübertragung historischer Ereignisse, insbesondere des Golfkriegs. Dieses semantische Zögern scheint mir charakteristisch für die Verwirrung der Wahrnehmung, die von nun an unsere Gesellschaftsformen berührt, angesichts der tele-technologischen Fortschritte und der abnehmenden Bedeutung der geometrischen Optik, der PASSIVEN OPTIK des materiellen Raumes (der Linse, des Wassers oder der Luft), die letztlich nichts anderes bewußt dokumentiert, als die unmittelbare Umgebung des Menschen. Wenn Sie einverstanden sind, nennen wir die letztgenannte Optik die *kleine Optik*, um uns für die Wellen- und Übertragungsoptik, die AKTIVE OPTIK des Zeitalters der Lichtgeschwindigkeit die Bezeichnung *große Optik* vorzubehalten, da diese ja weit über den klassischen Begriff des *Horizonts* hinausgeht. Es ist auch evident, daß die Elektro-Optik der Wellen, die das Signal VIDEO übermittelt, tatsächlich in die Frage nach der Digitalisierung dieses Signals einführt, über deren Wichtigkeit sich alle einig sind, nicht nur im Bereich der astronomischen Observation mit den Heldentaten einer sogenannten ‹adaptiven› Optik, sondern vor allem auch in der jüngsten *Realisierung der Räume virtueller Realität.* Da ja die Optik derjenige Bereich der Physik ist, der die Eigenheiten des Lichts und daher die Phänomene der Visualisation behandelt, gesellt sich zur Aufspaltung des Sehens auch noch die Aufspaltung des Lichts, nicht nur wie früher schon zwischen dem NATÜRLICHEN Licht (der Sonne) und dem KÜNSTLICHEN Licht (der Elektrizität) sondern außerdem zwischen dem DIREKTEN Licht (Sonne und Elektrizität) und dem INDIREKTEN Licht (der Videoüberwachung), die aus der Interaktion in Echtzeit von optischen und elektronischen Phänomenen hervorgeht – daher der Terminus OPTO.ELEKTRONIK. Das alles führt uns jetzt dahin, nicht mehr nur wie die Philosophen des klassischen Zeitalters von der *Ausdehnung* und der *Dauer* des materiellen Raumes zu sprechen, sondern auch von der *optischen Tiefe* der Lichtzeit und von seiner ‹opto-elektronischen› Steigerung, die das Einholen der geometrischen Perspektive der italienischen Renaissance durch eine elektronische Perspektive erfordert: die einer Echtzeit der Ausstrahlung und der augenblicklichen Rezeption der audio-video Signale.

So wohnen wir angesichts der jüngsten Erneuerung der *geometrischen* Optik der Lichtstrahlen durch die *Wellenoptik* ‹elektro-magnetischer› Strahlung von Partikeln, die die Vision und die Audition vermitteln, dem Auftauchen eines letzten Typus von Transparenz bei: *der Transparenz augenblicklicher Erscheinungen,* die auf/aus Distanz übertragen werden, TRANS.APPARENZ, die von nun an die natürliche Erscheinung der irdischen Athmosphäre vervollständigen wird und die im gleichen Zuge eine Art von ‹stereoskopischer› Verdopplung der sinnlichen Erscheinungen, der Darstellung der Welt und daher indirekt der Ästhetik selbst veranlaßt.

Zur Ästhetik der Erscheinung der Objekte und der Personen, die sich von dem Erscheinungshorizont der Einheit von Zeit und Ort der klassischen Perspektive abheben, kommt die Ästhetik des Verschwindens der fernen Personen hinzu, die in der *Abwesenheit des Horizonts* eines Fernsehbildschirms auftauchen, wo die Einheit der Zeit über die Einheit des Ortes des Zusammentreffens siegt: *die Perspektive der Echtzeit* der großen Optik verdrängt endgültig die Leistungen der kleinen Optik *der Perspektive des realen Raumes*; der Fluchtpunkt der Fokalisation der Lichtstrahlen überläßt plötzlich der Flucht aller Punkte (der Pixel) des Fernsehbildes den Vorrang.

Seither wird die *direkte* Transparenz des Raumes, die es einem jeden von uns erlaubt, seinen unmittelbaren Nachbarn wahrzunehmen, durch die *indirekte* Transparenz der Zeit der Geschwindigkeit der elektro-magnetischen Wellen ergänzt, die unsere Bilder, unsere Stimme und morgen – zweifeln wir nicht daran – dank eines bestimmten Datenkostüms (DATA SUIT), das nicht nur die Tele.vision oder die Tele.audition, sondern auch unsere wechselseitige AKTION überträgt – eine gemeinsame TELE.ACTION. Aber bevor wir uns mit dem Rahmen der zukünftigen TELE.EXISTENZ befassen, kommen wir, wenn Sie einverstanden sind, auf diese GROSSE elektromagnetische OPTIK zurück, die es uns heute erlaubt, uns *auf/aus Distanz wiederzutreffen*, an den Antipoden des Planeten.

Zur *direkten* Beleuchtung durch die Sonne, die die Aktivität unserer Jahre in voneinander unterschiedene Tage einteilt, kommt für uns von nun an die *indirekte* Beleuchtung hinzu, das ‹Licht› einer Technologie, die die Aufspaltung der Zeitpersönlichkeit begünstigt; eine Aufspaltung zwischen der Echtzeit unserer im Hier und Jetzt vollzogenen, unmittelbaren *Aktivitäten* und der Echtzeit einer vermittelten *Interaktivität*, die das ‹Jetzt› des Zeitraums der Fernsehsendung begünstigt, dem ‹Hier›, das heißt dem Raum des Treffpunktes, zum Schaden.

Wie aber wirklich leben, wenn es *Hier* nicht mehr gibt und wenn alles *Jetzt* ist? Und wie morgen überleben im augenblicklichen Ineinanderstoßen (téléscopage) einer ubiquitär gewordenen Realität, die sich in zwei gleichermaßen reale Zeiten zerlegt: diejenige der *Präsenz* des Hier und Jetzt und diejenige einer *Tele-Präsenz* auf Distanz, jenseits des Horizonts der sinnlichen Erscheinungen? Wie rational mit der Aufspaltung fertig werden, nicht nur mit der zwischen VIRTUELLER und AKTUELLER REALITÄT, sondern auch zwischen dem unmittelbar-sichtbaren, die Grenze der Wahrnehmung meiner gewohnten Aktivität *absteckenden* Horizont (horizon apparent) und dem *mittelbar-sichtbaren* Horizont eines Bildschirms, der plötzlich eine Art zeitliches Fenster öffnet, um anderswo und oft weit weg zu interagieren?

Es sei denn, man würde nach Art von Marvin MINSKY die Bedeutung der ‹analogen› Optik leugnen, und daher müssen wir vom sichtbaren Horizont aus von nun an unbedingt den STEREOSKOPISCHEN Charakter nicht nur des ‹Reliefs der Erscheinungen› und der dritten räumlichen Dimension befragen, sondern insbesondere auch die vierte des *zeitlichen Reliefs*, das dieses Mal durch die Aufspaltung zwischen den räumlichen und zeitlichen Nahabständen veranlaßt wird, Relief einer Welt, das von nun an von der elektro-optischen Amplifikation seiner Feldtiefe überbelichtet ist.

«Die Präsenz ist nur aus der Distanz Präsenz, und diese Distanz ist absolut, d.h. irreduzibel», schrieb Maurice BLANCHOT ... Heute, da der Begriff der Distanz in der Physik seinen Platz dem der ‹Kapazität› der augenblicklichen Ausstrahlung überlassen hat, führt die Wellenoptik zu einer ‹Fluktuation der Erscheinungen›, in der die Distanz nicht mehr, wie es der Poet wünschen würde, die Tiefe der Präsenz, sondern nur ihr Intermittieren ist. Das *Raumintervall* (negatives Zeichen) und das *Zeitintervall* (positives Zeichen) haben seit kurzem ihre Vorherrschaft dem Nullintervall der *Lichtgeschwindigkeit* der die Information übertragenden Wellen überlassen – kommen wir daher nun auf die Probleme zu sprechen, die durch die Erneuerung einer ‹Digitalisierung der Signale› (audio-video und taktil) gestellt werden, die nicht mehr wie früher mit der Ästhetik der

Erscheinungen eine Realisierung der REPRÄSENTATION der sinnlichen Realität, sondern gut und gern auch ihre unzeitige PRÄSENTATION erlauben, dank der Empfänger, Sensoren und anderer ‹Teledetektoren› aus dem Bereich, den wir TELEPRÄSENZ genannt haben.
Erinnern wir uns beiläufig auch noch, daß es auf der Welt kein echtes Dasein gibt – auf der wirklichen Welt sinnlicher Erfahrung – außer durch den Betrug der Ego-Zentrierung eines *gegenwärtig* Lebendigen, anders gesagt, durch die Existenz eines wirklichen Körpers, der im *Hier und Jetzt* lebt.
Die durch die intermittierende ‹Tele-Präsenz-auf-Distanz› aufgeworfene Frage führt also, mag dies den Kognitivisten auch mißfallen, in eine Reihe von Fragestellungen ein, die denen analog sind, die in der Physik durch den berühmten Begriff von Plancks Konstante gestellt wurden: wenn die extreme räumliche Entfernung plötzlich ihren Platz der extremen Nähe der Echtzeit des Austausches überläßt, *bleibt ein irreduzibler Spalt bestehen.*
Trotz der Abwesenheit des Intervalls, das auf die Inexistenz der Echtzeit des Zusammentreffens zurückgeht, verbietet das Interface des Nullzeichens der elektromagnetischen Wellen, das die TELEKOMMUNIKATION ermöglicht, die übliche Verwirrung des ‹Hier und Jetzt›; die Momentaufnahme der Interaktivität beseitigt niemals die Unterscheidung zwischen dem Akt und dem Agieren auf Distanz.
Es verhält sich im übrigen ebenso im Fall einer gemeinsamen TELE.EXISTENZ und dies unabhängig vom Grad der Nähe der in der Distanz vereinten Teleakteure.
So gibt es neben dem Gebrauch des Sichtgeräts (VPL) und des Datenkostüms im Bereich des virtuellen Raumes (CYBERSPACE), der eine erste Aufspaltung der Zeitpersönlichkeit in eine AKTUELLE und eine VIRTUELLE hervorbringt, auch ein anderes Verfahren dieses Typs *(elektro-ergonomischer)* Ausrüstung, die dieses Mal den aktuellen Raum des Austauschs auf Distanz betrifft: diejenige des TELEOPERATEURS

(oder, wenn man das vorzieht, der Telemanipulatoren), aufgrund des neuesten Fortschritts der TELE.TAKTILITÄT, wobei das ‹Höchstrelief› des Berührens auf Distanz die klangliche ‹Höchsttreue› und die visuelle ‹Höchstbestimmung› ergänzt.

Daher das zukünftige Auftauchen eines rein ‹zeitlichen› Volumens, also *das Erscheinen einer Perspektive des Berührens in Echtzeit,* die diejenige der klassischen Visualisation der Perspektivisten des Quattrocento erschüttert und damit die Vision der Welt des nächsten Jahrhunderts erschüttern wird.

Man wird tatsächlich bemerken, daß *die große Wellenoptik* sich nicht mehr nur mit der visuellen Tragweite befaßt, sondern daß sie die Gesamtheit der Wahrnehmung sinnlicher Erscheinungen nach sich zieht, den Tastsinn eingeschlossen, und dies: *weil die Zeit, die Echtzeit des dritten Intervalls dieser Art von Licht elektromagnetischer Wellen* über die Echtzeit der Materie, über ‹Ausdehnung›, über ‹Dauer› der Bestandteile, aus denen sich die enge menschliche Umgebung zusammensetzt, endgültig siegt.

Dank der heutigen sogenannten leistungsrückführenden Techniken, dank des Feed-back des TELETACT Handschuhs, der gerade kommerzialisiert wurde, und morgen dank der integralen teletaktilen Kombinationen, wo das Berühren, der Impakt, derjenige des ganzen Körpers sein wird, werden wir der industriellen Produktion einer Persönlichkeitsaufspaltung beiwohnen, nicht nur der Clonage des lebendigen Menschen, sondern der technischen Schöpfung eines der ältesten Mythen: dem Mythos des DOUBLE, einem spektral anwesenden, ‹elektroergonomischen› Double, eine andere Bezeichnung für das Phantom oder den Tot-Lebendigen. Es ist tatsächlich unmöglich, die diesem Genre neuer Technologien eigene Dramatik nicht heraufzubeschwören.

Das Geburtstrauma betrifft nicht nur das Kind, das Subjekt, sondern auch das Objekt, das auftauchende Instrument; wir müssen versuchen, die ‹Urszene› dieser Art technischer Neuerung aufzudecken. Wenn wir nicht absichtlich die *Erfindung des Schiffbruchs* mit der Erfindung des Schiffes oder des Zugunglücks mit der Erfindung der Eisenbahn vergessen, müssen wir das versteckte Gesicht dieser neuen Technologien befragen, bevor es sich uns ohne unser Wollen aufdrängt.

Schon der *Computervirus* erbringt eine erste Antwort auf die Frage der Negativität elektronischer Netze; erlauben Sie mir aber, Sie auf einen anderen Weg der Forschung zu führen, den der *ökologischen Verschmutzung*.

Verschmutzung, nicht nur die der atmosphärischen, der hydrosphärischen oder anderer ‹Substanzen›, sondern auch die bisher nicht wahrgenommene der ‹Distanzen›, diese DROMOSPHÄRISCHE Verschmutzung der Zeitabstände, setzen die Ausdehnung eines engen Planeten, der in der Leere des Alls hängt, auf ein nichts oder auf ein fast nichts herab.

Nachdem wir Erdlinge uns die schon so legitime Verschmutzung der NATUR bewußt gemacht haben, kommt es uns da nicht auch zu, uns daran zu machen, diese VERSCHMUTZUNG DER GRÖSSE NATUR zu untersuchen, die der Aufschwung der Echtzeittechnologien hervorgebracht hat?

Während die KLEINE GEOMETRISCHE OPTIK erlaubt, wahrzunehmen und daher die Eigenwelt als ‹Ausdehnung› und ‹Dauer›, d.h. als *geographische Größe* zu begreifen, dies dank der Weite des realen Raumes der Erscheinungen, löst umgekehrt die GROSSE OPTIK der Wellen heute die Geräumigkeit des menschlichen Milieus auf.

Da die Sendungs- und Rezeptionskapazität von verschiedenen Zeichen in Echtzeit die Natur der Zeitabstände verfremdet, nutzt sie die aktive Optik der elektromagnetischen *Wellen* der Feldtiefe aus, die Realität der wirklichen Welt, in dem Maße, daß sie auf nichts, oder fast nichts, reduziert wird, was dann von da aus zu einer katastrophalen Empfindung der Einkerkerung der Menschheit führt, die buchstäblich des Horizonts beraubt ist...

Tatsächlich, da, wo die kleine *passive* Optik des Raumes und

der Materie – der Luft, des Wassers, der Linsen – sich damit begnügt, die GROSSE WELT der Erscheinungen zu betrachten, öffnet sich die große *aktive* Optik des Zeitalters der Lichtgeschwindigkeit jenseits jeden Horizonts auf die aussetzende Wahrnehmung der KLEINEN WELT der Transparenz der Wellen, die verschiedene Signale trägt: ‹Transapparenz›, die die gewohnte Grenze der Horizontlinie abschafft zugunsten eines einzigen Rahmens, des Bildschirms; ‹viereckiger Horizont› einer Art von perspektivisch gespaltener Realität; STEREO. REALITÄT, wo die ‹Tiefen› und die ‹Höhen› des Klangreliefs der akustischen Höchsttreue einerseits durch die Schwere, das Gewicht des Körpers und damit der realen Distanzen einer *ganzen* Welt und andererseits durch die Abwesenheit von Gewicht, von Schwere, von Signalen einer Art von visueller und taktiler Höchst-Definition ersetzt würden, die in den exotischen Bereich elektromagnetischer Felder gehören.
Da die Größe Natur der *physikalischen Distanzen,* die so dem Gesetz der *mikrophysikalischen Gewalt* der Strahlen unterzogen wurden, die Audition, die Vision und morgen auch das Berühren (die Berührung-auf-Distanz) übertragen – wie da nicht das Risiko eines Verlusts der wirklichen Welt für die Menschheit heraufbeschwören? Und wie also nicht von nun an fürchten, daß auf den Menschen ein tiefes Gefühl der Eingeschlossenheit zukommt, der Eingeschlossenheit in einer Umgebung, die zugleich ihres Horizonts und ihrer *optischen Tiefe* beraubt ist?
Edgar Degas, dem man den romantischen Satz Amiels zitierte *«Eine Landschaft, das ist ein Seelenzustand»* konterte *«Nein, das ist ein Augenzustand».* Heute, wo man sich mit dem Gleichgewicht der menschlichen Umgebung, die sehr stark von der industriellen Zerstörung bedroht wird, beschäftigt, sollte sich da nicht zur Sorge um die GRÜNE ÖKOLOGIE diejenige um eine GRAUE ÖKOLOGIE, die sich für die postindustrielle Herabstufung der Feldtiefe der irdischen Landschaft interessieren würde, hinzugesellen?

Die Raumsonde PIONEER 10, die vor 20 Jahren, am 2. März 1972 in den Weltraum entlassen wurde, ist das erste von Menschenhand hergestellte Objekt, das das Sonnensystem verlassen hat, aber es ist auch, vielleicht vor allem, *eine Art von Maßstab für verschiedene kosmische Größen*. Irgendwo in *8 Milliarden Kilometern Entfernung von der Erde*, strahlt die amerikanische Rakete jeden Tag Signale aus, die *7 Stunden 30 Minuten* brauchen, um die Antennen der NASA zu erreichen. Da das Teleskop und alle Instrumente an Bord der Sonde funktionsfähig bleiben, entspricht die ‹Echtzeit› der von PIONEER übermittelten Botschaften also praktisch der Zeitverschiebung zwischen TOKIO und PARIS ...
Als wirklicher elektronischer Empfänger der Weite des Universums unterrichtet uns die Raumsonde so ständig und durch ein nur leicht verschobenes Feed-back über die fortschreitende Einschränkung der irdischen Ausdehnung.
Wenn es tatsächlich so ist, wie Gustave Flaubert es beschreibt, daß, «je besser die Teleskope werden, es desto mehr Sterne geben wird», so läßt er noch die Auswirkungen dieser plötzlichen optischen Erweiterung aus: *je mehr die Wahrnehmung des Jenseits der Welt entwickelt sein wird, umso weniger wird es von der Welt, der ganzen Erde, geben*. Je mehr die Mittel verbessert sein werden, die es erlauben, das Jenseits des Horizonts zu kennen, desto mehr wird die irdische Ausdehnung, die ‹Dauer› der Welt der sinnlichen Erfahrung verflacht, auf nichts, auf weniger als nichts reduziert – das, was man umgangssprachlich *das andere Ende des Opernglases* nennt.
Bemerken wir nebenbei, daß, wenn die kleine geometrische Optik früher mit Galilei den Menschen von neuem gezeigt hatte, daß die ERDE SICH DREHT, die große elektronische Optik sich daran macht, zu zeigen, daß das UNIVERSUM SICH AUSDEHNT ... zwei Zeiten, zwei Zeitalter der Wahrnehmung und zwei radikal verschiedene ‹Bewegungen›.
Aber kommen wir auf unsere Raumsonde zurück, die dazu bestimmt ist, aus der Nähe die Sterne des Sonnensystems zu

beobachten, vor allem JUPITER. Vorwärtsgetrieben von der Gravitationskraft dieses Planeten, folgt die amerikanische Rakete unerbittlich ihrer Bahn ins Unendliche mit einer *Geschwindigkeit von 46.000 Kilometern in der Stunde.* Aber um welche STUNDE und um welchen KILOMETER handelt es sich, da sich die Sonde ja seit 20 Jahren von jedem geographischen Bezugspunkt entfernt hat? So isoliert, ist die automatische Sonde in der Tat *nirgendwo*, sodaß die Menschen, die ihren Abschuß gesichert haben und die heute in Rente sind, wie B.J. O'Brien, erklären: «Das ist beeindruckend, *das ist sogar zum verrückt werden.*»

Trotz des rationalen, wissenschaftlichen Aspekts dieses Gesetzes der *universellen Erweiterung*, das vor fast 60 Jahren von Edwin Hubble und einigen anderen eröffnet wurde, schätzt nichts und niemand wirklich die Auswirkungen dieser Bewegung auf die gewohnte Wahrnehmung, auf die unmittelbare Erfahrung ein, während ein großes Phänomen der Anziehung, des Ansaugens heute die Auswirkung der irdischen Erscheinungen absorbiert. Mit der Verflüchtigung der berühmten ‹Ozonschicht› allzu beschäftigt, nimmt noch keiner von uns die fortschreitende Entrealisierung des iridischen Horizonts wahr, diese andere Verflüchtigung, die aus der zukünftigen Vorherrschaft der REALEN ZEITPERSPEKTIVE der Wellenoptik über die des realen Raumes der geometrischen Optik des QUATTROCENTO hervorgeht; und daher wird ‹BIG.-VIEW› dennoch logischerweise den gefeierten BIG.BANG der zeitgenössischen Astrophysik vervollständigen.

Man kann sich heute mit Recht fragen, ob Edwin Hubble, einer der Gründerväter des *Prinzips der kosmischen Erweiterung* (insbesondere dank der Leistungen des Teleskops von Mont Wilson) nicht 1929 das erste Opfer der von Flaubert angekündigten optischen Illusion war, wie es im übrigen Albert Einstein seinerzeit vermutete ... Was die jüngsten Apostel des BIG. BANG angeht – auch sie könnten ohne weiteres die Opfer des Dekors einer astronomischen Transparenz sein, die durch die

Übertragungsgeschwindigkeit der Signale der Teleskope oder der Radioteleskope angewachsen ist.
Optische Vergrößerung, optische Verkleinerung, Dopplereffekt der Verschiebung hin zu rot im Spektrum der Galaxien, andere Bezeichnungen der Beschleunigung und Verlangsamung der Erscheinungen, wo die DROMOSKOPIE – Lichtgeschwindigkeitsenergie – *buchstäblich die wahrnehmbare Realität beleuchtet*, eine Realität, deren STEREOSKOPISCHES RELIEF schon eine Reihe von Verwirrungen in der Wahrnehmung hervorruft, die man, glaube ich, schließlich doch berücksichtigen müßte, da ja selbst der Begriff der ‹physikalischen Nähe› Gefahr läuft, radikal geändert zu werden. Die GROSSE OPTIK erlaubt es, die weiteste astrophysische Entfernung zu testen, aber sie trägt umgekehrt auch dazu bei, die nächste physikalische Nähe in Zweifel zu ziehen. Beobachten wir als Bestätigung, daß die Verantwortlichen vor 20 Jahren, bevor sie die Raumsonde PIONEER starteten, es für gut hielten, auf der Rakete eine Identitätsplakette anzubringen, überdies die Darstellung des Sonnensystems und die Silhouetten eines Mannes und einer Frau. Um den möglichen Außerirdischen eine Idee von unseren Dimensionen zu vermitteln, fügten die Amerikaner ein Wasserstoffatom hinzu: *der Abstand zwischen dem Kern und seinem einzigen Elektron definiert eine Maßeinheit*. Obgleich die Sonde, die gestartet werden sollte, dazu bestimmt war, die Maßlosigkeit der kosmischen Ausdehnung zu erforschen, haben die Wissenschaftler so auch dem Begriff der ‹minimalen Distanz› seine Funktion als Maßstab für die GRÖSSE NATUR wiedergegeben, die ja nun tatsächlich unsere erste Wohnstatt ist. Ob man es nun will oder nicht, für jeden von uns gibt es jetzt die Spaltung der Darstellung (représentation) der Welt und daher ihrer REALITÄT. Aufspaltung zwischen Aktivität und Interaktivität, Präsenz und Telepräsenz, Existenz und Tele-Existenz. Mit dem STEREOSKOPISCHEN Charakter eines Realen konfrontiert, das sich in Optik und Elektrooptik, Akustik und Elektroakustik, Berührung und

Tele-Taktilität aufteilt, sind wir gezwungen, unsere Seh- und Denkgewohnheiten aufzugeben, um einen neuen Typ von ‹Relief› aufzufassen, der den praktischen Nutzen des Begriffs des HORIZONTS und damit die ‹Perspektive›, die es uns bis heute erlaubt hat, uns im *Hier und Jetzt* zu bestätigen, wieder in Frage stellt. Und dies alles, weil die frühere einzige ‹Licht›- und damit ‹Realitäts›quelle sich gespalten hat; da nun der direkte Schatten der Sonnenstrahlen oder der elektrischen Lampe von den indirekten ‹Schattenzonen› der Abwesenheit der Ausstrahlung elektronischer Signale ergänzt wird, da die TELEÜBERWACHUNG plötzlich die Beleuchtung der Dinge verdrängt, die Wahrnehmung das Mit-eigenen-Augen-sehen des gewöhnlichen Beobachters. Als erste Generation der Geschichte wohnen wir der Eroberung des Weltraumes, aber vor allem der Eroberung einer Geschwindigkeit bei, die die Inbesitznahme der Echtzeit der Augenblicklichkeit ermöglicht, wir wohnen aber auch der Enthüllung einer der letzten Energieformen bei: der KINEMATISCHEN ENERGIE, Energie ‹in Bildern› oder, wenn man das vorzieht, ‹in Informationen›, die so den potentiellen und kinetischen Energien hinzugefügt werden. Dritte Energieform, die nicht nur die GEOMETRISIERUNG der Vision der Welt ermöglicht, geradeso wie die der Perspektivisten der italienischen Renaissance, sondern auch ihre INDUSTRIALISIERUNG; das Handwerk der von den Vertretern der ‹passiven› Optik des Raums und der Materie ausgearbeiteten Erscheinungen tritt ihren Platz der Industrie der ‹aktiven› (elektro-optischen) Optik des Zeitalters der Lichtgeschwindigkeit ab. Tatsächlich – wenn der zeitgenössische Relativist der Ära Einsteins den Begriff der physikalischen ‹Distanz› durch den der ‹Kapazität› der Sendung und der augenblicklichen mikrophysikalischen Rezeption ersetzt, vernichtet er im gleichen Zug die alte Vorherrschaft der perspektivistischen Konzeption des galileischen Zeitalters – er fügt sogar ein drittes Intervall vom Typ ‹Licht› den klassischen Intervallen vom Typ ‹Raum› und vom Typ ‹Zeit› hinzu. Er bewirkt eine Veränderung

des Prinzips der Realität, wo der AUTOMATISCHE Charakter der Darstellungen der Normalisierung der Wahrnehmung entspricht, die der Gebrauch der synthetisierenden Energie der elektronischen Bilder erlaubt und dies im ‹analogen› ebenso wie im ‹numerischen› Bereich.
Bemerken wir zum Schluß, daß die TELEPRÄSENZ in der Perspektive und daher die gemeinsame TELE.EXISTENZ jenseits der Grenzen der gewohnten Nähe nicht nur die ‹Linie› des Erscheinungshorizonts zugunsten der Abwesenheit der tiefen und imaginären Horizontlinie abschafft, sondern daß sie den Begriff des RELIEF selbst wieder in Frage stellt; das Berühren, die BERÜHRUNG AUF DISTANZ verwirrt nämlich nicht nur die Unterscheidung zwischen ‹aktuell› und ‹virtuell›, wie es heute die Adepten des CYBERSPACE erklären, sondern selbst die Realität des NAHEN und des FERNEN, die ihrerseits unsere Präsenz im *Hier und Jetzt* in Frage stellt und die von dieser Tatsache die Bedingungen der Notwendigkeit sinnlicher Erfahrung abkoppelt.

Übersetzung aus dem Französischen von Antje Quast

Paul Virilio
Big Optics

«Lo, there shall be more stars as telescopes get more and more perfect» *(Gustave Flaubert)*

I would like to talk to you about splitting vision and the emergence of a second kind of optics: the kind that today lets TELECONFERENCES take place between Tokyo and Paris.
It is now some years ago that certain people were describing this phenomenon as A HOLE IN SPACE, others, still more recently as A HOLE IN TIME, in the real time of instantaneous live transmission of historic events, particularly the Gulf War. To me, this semantic hesitancy seems to be characteristic of the troubled perception that now affects our society when faced with tele-technological progress and the decline of the importance of geometrical optics, passive optics of space taken up by matter (glass, water, or air), and which after all accounts only for man's own immediate environs.
If you wish, we might call the latter *small optics* in order to reserve for the undulatory optics of the air waves the term *big optics*, the ACTIVE OPTICS of time passing at the speed of light, as this reaches out beyond our classical notion of *the horizon*.
It is also evident that the electro-optics of air waves serving as vehicle for a video signal in fact leads on to the question of digitalization of that signal. Of that everyone, of course, claims awareness, not just as regards the value of so called ‹adaptive› optics in the field of astronomical observation, but above all for the recent achievement of *spaces of virtual reality*.
Since optics consists of the part of physics dealing with the properties of light and hence the phenomena of visualization,

it follows that with the splitting-up of vision light itself must also be split; not just as before into NATURAL light (the sun) and artificial light (electricity), but also into DIRECT (both sun and electricity) and INDIRECT light (closed circuit tv surveillance) which results in real time interaction between both optical phenomena and electronic ones, hence the term OPTO-ELECTRONICS.

All this leads us now to talk not just like the classical philosophers about the *area* and *expanse* of matter space, but also about the *optical depth* of light time and its ‹opto-electronic› amplification which compels us to replace the geometric perspective of the Italian Renaissance with an electronic perspective: that of real time transmission and instantaneous reception of audio and video signals.

Thus, with the recent rejuvenation of *geometric* light ray optics through *undulatory* optics of ‹electro-magnetic› particle radiation which transmits both visual and aural impulses we are witnessing the emergence of a latest type of transparency: *the transparency of appearances instantly transmitted across large distances*, a TRANS-APPARENCY which has consequently come to in a way complement the natural transparency of the terrestrial atmosphere, giving rise at the same time to a kind of ‹stereoscopic› reduplication of any perceptible appearances, the representation of the world and hence indirectly even of aesthetics themselves.

The aesthetics of appearance, according to which objects or people stand out against an *apparent horizon* of a unity of time and space as in classical perspective, is supplemented by aesthetics of disappearance of someone in the distance suddenly rising up on the horizonless screen of the cathode-ray tube, the unity of time transferring such aesthetics onto that particular space of encounter: this is *real time perspective* of big optics clearly supplanting the achievements of the small optics of a *perspective of real space*, the vanishing point of focussed light rays suddenly giving way to the primacy of the vanishing of all the points (pixels) of the televized image.

Henceforth the *direct* transparency of space which enables any of us to perceive their immediate neighbours is complemented by the *indirect* transparency of time taken by the speed of electro-magnetic waves transmitting our images, voices, and, by tomorrow no doubt reciprocal actions, too, thanks to the DATA-SUIT which will allow not just tele-vision or tele-audition, but also communal TELE-ACTION.

But before tackling the framework for a future TELE-EXISTENCE let us come back to electromagnetic BIG OPTICS which today allows us to *join, from great distances*, at the Antipodes of the planet.

Meanwhile, in additon to *direct* light from the sun which divides the passing of our active years into distinct days, we get *indirect* lighting, the ‹light› of a technology that encourages a sort of split of the characteristics of time into real time of *immediate action* where we act at one and the same time *both* here *and* now, and real time of a *mediated interactivity* which privileges the ‹now› of the hourly presentation of the televized emission to the detriment of the ‹here›, i.e. the actual space of encounter.

How can you really live if *here* is no more and everything is *now*? How to survive tomorrow with an instantaneous telescopic view of a reality that has become ubiquitous and breaks down into two equally real times: that of *presence* here and now, and that of the *tele-presence* over a distance from beyond the horizon of sensory-perceptible material appearances?

How do we manage this split rationally, having to differentiate not just between ACTUAL and VIRTUAL REALITIES, but also between an *apparent* horizon which marks the perceptive limits of my customary activity, and the *trans-apparent* horizon of a screen that suddenly opens up a sort of temporal window through which to interact somewhere else and often very far away?

In order to negate, in the words of Marvin MINSKY, the significance of ‹analogue› optics and thus the horizon of material appearances it is imperative for us to investigate the STEREO-

SCOPIC character not just of the ‹relief of material appearances› and the third spatial dimension, but above all the fourth dimension, the *temporal relief* this time occasioned by a split between spatial and temporal proximities, the relief of a world now overexposed through the electro-optical amplification of the deepest and darkest recesses of its landscape.

«Presence is only presence at a distance, and this distance must be absolute, that is to say unyielding», wrote Maurice BLANCHOT ...

Today, as the notion of ‹distance› has given way in physics for one of a form of ‹energy› released at the moment of instantaneous emission, undulatory optics has resulted in a ‹fluctuation of appearances›, where distance no longer reveals the profundities of presence so yearned for by the poet, but only its intermittency. As the unit intervals of *space* (negative) and *time* (positive) have ceded very little of their primacy to the unit interval of zero designation of the *speed of light* of information transmitting waves, let us now come to the problems posed by the innovation of the ‹digitalization of signals› (audio-visual and tactile), achieving not just as in former times the REPRESENTATION of the reality of sensory perception with the help of the aesthetics of material appearance, but well and truly its untimely PRESENTATION, thanks to the captors for the senses and other ‹tele-detectors› of what is called TELE-PRESENCE.

Let us remember briefly that there is no real existence in this world – in the real world of sensory perception – except by the delusory device provided by the ego-centrism of the *live presence*, that is the existence of a real body living *here and now*.

The question of intermittent ‹tele-presence-at-a-distance› therefore introduces, without wanting to cause insult with cognitive science, a series of problems analogous to those set in physics by PLANCK'S famous DISTANCE: When extreme distance suddenly yields to extreme proximity of real time exchange, *there nevertheless remains an irreducible gap*.

Though lacking an interval owing to the non-existence of real space for the encounter, the interface of the zero-sign of electromagnetic waves providing TELECOMMUNICATION nevertheless prohibits the habitual confusion involved when mingling ‹here and now›, the instantaneousness of interaction never quite manages to eliminate the distinction between the actual act itself and acting at a distance.
The same applies elsewhere; namely in the case of a communal TELE-EXISTENCE, where it would fit the degree of proximity between various tele-actors joined together over a wide distance.
Thus, besides the application of the VPL (data visor) and the DATASUIT in the virtual expanse of CYBERSPACE which provokes an initial personality split between ACTUAL/REAL time and VIRTUAL time, there is also another application for that kind of *electro-ergonomic* equipment, this time dealing with the real space of exchange at a distance: the space of the TELE-OPERATOR (or, if you prefer, tele-manipulator) created by recent progress in the development of TELE-TACTILITY or ‹high relief› long distance touch impact which would supplement aural ‹high fidelity› and visual ‹high definition›.
It will lead to the emergence of a purely ‹temporal› volume unit and therefore the *advent of a perspective of real time touch impact* which will come to overturn the linear perspective of classical visualization of the Quattrocento, and thus revolutionize our view of the world in the next century.
You will have noticed that *big undulatory optics* are in effect no longer linked to just a visual context, but incorporate the entire range of perceiving sensory perception including the sense of touch. And: this is so *because time, the real time of the third interval of the lightning kind of electromagnetic waves* has taken big optics into the real space of matter, the ‹area› and ‹expanse› of the substances that make up the human environment.
Thanks to the technological development of certain interactive

feed-back techniques, such as the TELETACTILITY of the data glove now available commercially, and a comprehensive teletactile combination where touch and impact will tomorrow involve the entire body, we shall witness the industrial production of the split persona, not by cloning human beings, but through the technological recreation of one of the most ancient myths: that of the DOUBLE, an ‹electro-ergonomic› double as spectral presence, another invocation of the phantom figure of the living dead.

It is in fact impossible not to recount the drama of the plot appropriate to these kinds of new technologies.

As *the trauma of birth* affects not only the infant, the subject, but also the object and the emerging instrument we must attempt to discover ‹the original accident› specific to this particular technological innovation.

Although it is easy enough to forget the *invention of shipwreck* inherent in sailing, or the derailment built into the advent of the railways, we must nonetheless inquire after the hidden face of new technologies in order to prevent the former from surfacing and imposing on us to our own detriment.

Viral contamination has already been the first response as to the negativity of electronic circuitry, but let me lead you down another path of investigation: that of *ecological pollution*.

A pollution not merely of atmospheric, hydrospheric etc. ‹substances›, but an imperceptible pollution of ‹distances›, the DROMOSPHERIC pollution of time distances which reduces to next to nothing the scale of an already cramped planet suspended in sidereal emptiness.

Now, with our consciousness raised for the pollution of NATURE, would it not be appropriate for us terrestrians to apply ourselves equally to a study of the pollution of NATURE'S GRANDEUR as caused by the rise of real time technologies.

SMALL OPTICS of linear geometrics had enabled us to perceive, and thus to conceive of the world proper as an ‹area› and ‹expanse›, that is in terms of *geographic grandeur*, thanks to the very vastness of the real space of material appearances, whereas undulatory BIG OPTICS are today reducing the scope of the human environment.

If the power of real time transmission and reception of various signals is alienating nature from time distances, then the active optics of electro-magnetic waves exploit the depth of the landscape, in fact the very reality of the actual World, to the point of reducing it to nothing or next to nothing, and finally leaving mankind literally deprived of horizons with a catastrophic feeling of confinement.

In effect, where the *passive* small optics of material space – such as air, water, cut glass for optical lenses – was content to present the GREAT WORLD of appearances for your contemplation the *active* big optics of the speed of light are unleashed (from beyond any horizon) onto the intermittent perception of the SMALL WORLD made transparent by waves carrying their various signals: a ‹trans-apparency› that eliminates any customary line of horizon in favour of the boxed screen; a ‹horizon of the box› of some sort of split perspective reality; a STEREO REALITY where the ‹highs› and ‹lows› of the aural profile of high fidelity acoustics will be replaced partially by gravity – bodily weight and therefore real distances of a world still *intact* – and on the other hand by the kind of visual and tactile high-definition signals lacking in weightiness and gravity which inscribe themselves on the exotic terrain of electro-magnetic fields.

With nature's grandeur as embodied in *physical distances* thus submitted to the laws of *micro-physical power* of waves transmitting sound, vision, and tomorrow touch (long distance impact), how can you not conjure up a risk for mankind of losing its grip on the actual world? Moreover, how can you not, as of now dread the advent of a deep feeling of confinement of man locked in an environment at once deprived of horizon and of *optical depth?*

The French painter Edgar Degas, when quoted Amiel's romantic pronouncement *«a landscape, that is a state of one's spirit»* merely retorted, *«no, it's a state of the eyes!»*
Today as we worry about the equilibrium of a human world threatened by industrial dejection, would it not be apt to add to the concerns of a GREEN ECOLOGY those of a GREY ECOLOGY which would deal with the post industrial degredation of our most fundamental conception of the surface of Earth's landscape?
Launched twenty years ago on 2 March 1972 the space probe PIONEER 10 was the first man-made object to leave the solar system, but it also become a *sort of measuring stick for different cosmic scales.*
Situated somewhere *8 billion kilometres from earth* the American space craft every day transmitted signals which took *7 hours and thirty minutes* to reach the antennae of NASA. When the telescope and the entire array of instruments on board were operational the ‹real time› of the messages transmitted by PIONEER was therefore practically equivalent to the time difference between TOKYO and PARIS ...
As a true electronic captor of the vastness of the universe the space probe serves as a permanent reminder with its feed-back that is only slightly displaced in time of the progressive limitation of earthly size.
If indeed there «should be more stars as telescopes get more and more perfect», as Gustave Flaubert wrote, then he has omitted to also consider the consequence from this sudden optical dilation: *the further developed our perception of the otherworld is getting so there will be less of a world, of earth as a whole.*
The more our means of reconnoitering beyond the horizon are being perfected and with them our ability to reach out from earth, the more the ‹expanse› of the world as perceived by the senses will be limited, reduced to nil and less than nil. It is what is commonly known as looking through *the wrong end of the opera-glasses!*

In the course of this investigation let us note that initially the small optics of linear geometry could scarcely be illustrated by Galileo as he explained to man once more that the EARTH SPINS. In a way the link to the big optics of electronics could lie in their revelation of a DILATING UNIVERSE ... two ‹times›, two perceptive epochs, and two radically different ‹movements›.

But let us come back to our space probe destined to observe the stars of the solar system closely, particularly JUPITER. Propelled by the gravitational force of that planet the American space craft inexorably pursued its course into infinty at a speed of *46 000 kilometres an hour.* However, with what kind of HOUR and KILOMETRE are we dealing here, since the probe has been moving away from any geographical reference for 20 years? Out on its own the automated probe is in fact *nowhere*, so much so that men such as B.J. O'Brien who had assured its launch and are now in retirement are declaring: «It is impressive, *it could almost make you go crazy!*»

In spite of the rational and scientific aspects of this law of *universal expansion* found nearly sixty years ago by Edwin Hubble and a few others no one seems to really appreciate its effects on customary experience, on immediate experience, now that a strong phenomenon of attraction and suction is today absorbing the effect of the reality of terrestrial appearances.

Preoccupied by the disappearance of the famous ozone layer still no one amongst us seems to realize the progressive derealization of the terrestrial horizon, the other ‹disappearance› resulting in an impending primacy of REAL TIME PERSPECTIVE of undulatory optics over real space of the linear geometrical optics of the QUATTROCENTO. BIG VIEW that is nevertheless going to accomplish the renowned BIG BANG of contemporary astrophysics.

You may legitimately ask today if Edwin Hubble, as one of the founding fathers of the *principle of cosmic dilation* (mainly thanks to the high performance of the telescope at Mount

Wilson) had not in 1929 become the first victim of the optical illusion predicted by Flaubert, as Einstein also seemed to suspect at the time ... As for the recent apostles of the BIG BANG theory, they too might well have fallen prey to the décor of an astronomic transparency accrued through the speed of transmission of signals by telescopes or radio telescopes.

Optical enlargement or shrinkage, the double effect achieved when we take off into the red spectre of the galaxies, and new other units of acceleration or deceleration are all manifestations where Dromoscopics – the study of the light-energy of speed – *is literally illuminating the limits of perceptible reality*, a reality whose STEREOSCOPIC PROFILE is already giving rise to so many problems of perception that I do think we must pause to reflect, since the very notion of ‹physical proximity› is at risk of being altered radically. However, with BIG OPTICS permitting spectacular insights into the vastest astrophysical distances, it is nevertheless also contributing to the invalidation of the closest physical proximity.

Note that, almost in confirmation of my proposals, twenty years ago before launching the space probe PIONEER, those responsible thought it fitting to attach an identity plate to the craft. Besides depicting a configuration of the solar system with the planet earth and the silhouettes of a man and a woman the Americans included an atom of hydrogen in order to give any extra-terrestrians an impression of our dimensions: *the distance between the nucleus and its only electron was to define one unit of measurement.*

Now, although the craft about to be launched was meant to test the limits of cosmic dilation the scientists thus gave the notion of ‹minimal distance› back its function as evaluation of NATURE'S GRANDEUR which indeed should be our prime habitat.

Like it or not, we are now every one of us faced with a split representation of the world and hence of its REALITY; a split into activity and interactivity, presence and tele-presence, existence and tele-existence.

Confronted with the STEREOSCOPIC character of reality now shared by optics and electro-optics, acoustics and electro-acoustics, touch and tele-tactility, we are ready to abandon our ways of seeing and thinking in order to embrace a new type of ‹relief› which once more puts into doubt even the practical use of the notion of a horizon, and therefore the ‹perspective› which has so far enabled us to find our bearings and acknowledge we exist *here and now*.

All this has happened because the only source of ‹light› and, therefore, ‹reality› of former times has itself been split up. (Direct) shade from the rays of sunlight and the electric lightbulb has combined into dark ‹zones of (indirect) shade› not lit by the emission of electronic signals. Suddenly closed circuit television has arrived to supplant the illumination of things, the perception by sight from the eyes of the normal beholder.

As the first generation in history to witness the conquest of space and above all the mastery of a speed which allows the conquest of the real time of instantaneousness we are also witness to the discovery of the latest type of energy: CINEMATIC ENERGY, an energy ‹of images› or if you prefer ‹information› is thus added to the other two forms of energy, potential and kinetic.

It is this third type of energy which makes possible not only the GEOMETRISATION of our view of the world in the manner of the perspectivists of the Italian Renaissance, but also the INDUSTRIALISATION of that view, the manufacturing of appearances, value-added under the tenets of an industry of ‹active› optics (electro-optics) of illuminated time which is replacing the ‹passive› optics of material space.

If, in effect, the contemporary adherent of Einstein's theory of relativity were to replace the notion of physical ‹distance› with that of a ‹capacity› of instantaneous microphysical transmission and reception and at the same time eliminate the ancient supremacy of perspective perception of Galileo's era – then adding a third unit-measurement of ‹light› to the traditional ones

of ‹time› and ‹space› – he would obtain a mutation of the principle of reality, where the AUTOMATED character of representation would become equivalent to a normalized perception. This would come about through the use of the energy of synthesis of electronic imagery, generated in both the areas of ‹analogue› and ‹digital› representation.
To sum up, let us say that perspective TELE-PRESENCE and therefore a communal TELE-EXISTENCE from beyond the limitations of customary conceptions of proximity is not just eliminating the ‹line› of an actual apparent horizon in favour of an absence even of any deeper, imaginary line of horizon, but it would also dispose of the very notion of high profile RELIEF, of touch, as LONG DISTANCE TACTILITY will seriously upset not only the distinction between ‹actual› and ‹virtual› as already explained by the adepts of CYBERSPACE, but furthermore it would seriously challenge the very reality of NEAR and FAR, thus questioning our own presence *here and now*, which would seriously affect the conditions of necessity for direct sensual sensory experience.

Translated from the French original by J. von Stein

Avital Ronell
Support Our Tropes II (Or Why in Cyburbia There Are a Lot of Cowboys)

This is part of an ongoing reflection on the technologically constellated state, the Gulf War, and the prosthetic subject. In SOT I (Support our Tropes I), I explained the linguistic warping of «support our troops» who should be supporting us, and how this inversion, or chiasmus, implicated the entire population. This belongs to a fascistic notion of war in which the theater of warfare is deflected from the mobilization of troops toward the psychologistic or propagandistic control of the homefront. This signalled yet another deflection. What does it mean to resorb the home into the theater of operations by making it into a front? In the time allotted, I can only offer a few aphoristic statements, which I will try to present as clearly as possible, with a view to the discussion to which such theses ineluctably lead. At the same time I do not want to renounce the complexity that thinking has to engage if it is to fulfill its contract with itself. War is a strain on all of us; thinking accompanies the strain, reproducing genuine ennervation, anxiety, and the sense of not knowing where we are. It is to this twilight zone between knowing and not knowing that I commit myself because the upperhand (which is not yours or mine) has acted as if it knew where we are going and thus, implicitly, where we have been. This involves, among other things, *the psychotopologies of everyday life.*

«Now, where were we?» says the scholar. My assignment concerns Virtual Reality, media and the War in the Gulf. I do not feel that I master the materials, or even the immaterials (VR opens the question of immateriality) – I do not feel that I possess the mastery required to transmit knowledge properly or to produce linkage. Yet this assignment is about mastery and I consider myself an infomaniaque. VR is philosophically complex even though it is a system dependent on classical tropes of representation, imagination, the sovereign subject and negated otherness (negated otherness is what Hegel called the enemy). So it is dependent on a number of metaphysical cravings, but then who isn't? Might as well face it: there has always been a desire to transcend the body, and I have often said that I would donate my own body to science fiction. But the donation of a body in life is part of a metaphysical striving toward an indeterminate elsewhere. VR is jamming the master codes of this historical desire for transcendence and exteriority, and deserves to be heard out in all its effusions. Because VR is also about Being-in-the-world, and liberating the location of being to nonsubstantial spaces, it is trying to reconfigure the possibilities for sharing the world. According to Jaron Lanier, Howard Rheingold and others, VR practices a politics of finitude[1], and demands an *ethics of technology*. At the same time, however, VR is jacking into Mattel Corporation, the military and NASA but it is also a design testing ground for architecture and the medical sciences. So, where were we? asks the scholar. A rigorous study of virtual reality cannot be made to fit entirely into the frame of this event, but I will try to raise some questions to indicate the direction of my reflections on this difficult topic.

Virtual Reality, artificial reality, dataspace or cyberspace are inscriptions of a desire whose principal symptom can be seen as absence of community. Lanier's discourse has everything to do with the possibilities of constituting an ecstatic community that would refuse to be governed by a goal or a totalitarian drive toward unification. It is as if Lanier were tempted to retrieve

Bataille's community of shattered egos. To a certain extent, the metaphysical subject is broken up and displaced to routes of splintering disidentification. The subject no longer finds its mooring in identification with a substantial image. Still, Lanier, like all transmitters on behalf of radio VR (VR is said to be more like a telephone or radio, disconnected from the televisual apparatus), emphasizes the ego-building prowess of VR designs. This is a double-edged claim that we need to probe with unrelenting clarity. In cyburbia there is always a risk of blurring the distinction between simulation and the operational world. I am not convinced, though others are, that this entails a very new risk. More seriously perhaps, there is still a tendency to retrofit the technological prosthesis to a metaphysical subject: the sovereign subject of history, destiny's co-pilot. In other words, the technological prostheses would merely be an amplifier and intensifier borrowed by a centered subject whose fragmentation is, as they say, a simulation – that is, a device for *disavowing* fragmentation, self loss or, on another register, castration. This aspect of disavowal in part explains why Lanier, for his part, would have preferred to see VR called, as he asserts, ‹Intentional Reality›. Now this exposes a whole problematics of the intentional consciousness that I will address momentarily. The intentional consciousness is a philosophical construct that emerges when it is felt that we are not in control of our actions. And this is precisely where Lanier's project takes hold, in the control rooms of his majesty the Ego. In addition to arguing that VR is «good for the ego», he launches an assault against the contemporary subject's passivity; this assault on passivity – quite understandable at first sight – is however made in the dubious name of action and control.[2] The subject will take control. The argument against passivity, which I can only graze swiftly, is, I believe, a false and highly problematic one, though I also agree with the need to activate radical creativity. But the opposition of passive and active proffers a deluded equation. Take a look around you. Haven't we, as a culture been *too* active, *too* action

filled, even if action splits itself into representations of the traumatized spectator and manic warrior? Any uninterrogated invention made in the name of action has got to attract our deepest suspicions, girls and boys. *A true ethics of community, be it located in cyberspace or among lovers, readers, artists, activists and so on, would have to locate a passivity beyond passivity* – a space of repose and reflection, a space that would let the other come. Exposing oneself to the other, or to the other's death, has nothing to do with action as such. I'll elaborate this shortly. It is because of an articulated desire for action that cyberspace is also west of the west, that is, a memorex cowboy frontier.
One of the errors that Lanier makes is to say that «ultimately, everything is done by people and technology is only a little game that we play».[3] The war has shown us that people do not play little games. Nor is technology zoned outside of us, but as cybernetics and AI have shown, man-machinic hybridizations involve a refashioning of the human being, following a trajectory of altogether new alignments of self and the technobody. Now, the body, from Marvin Minsky onwards, has been devalorized into the «bloody mess of organic matter». I am not an essentialist feminist, but I do think that this utterance could never have been made by a woman, who takes out monthly mortgages on her body in the form of periodic bloodbaths and PMS (Premenstrual Stress). This is being said too quickly, perhaps, but it is urgent to recognize that the body of a woman has a fundamental relationship to death, despair, to finitude – and life. While the woman's body produces the eternal return of the «bloody mess of organic matter», the cyborg soldier, located in command and control systems, exercises on the fields of denial. Intentional Reality eliminates the body as organic, finite, damagable, eviscerable, castratable, crushable entity, thus closing off the orifices and stemming leakage and excrement. We are not very far from Deleuze and Guattari's BwO: the body-without-organs. Orificial shutdown and excremental control help explain why this war was conducted under the compulsive sign

of cleanliness: on the American side of language usage, this was a clean war, a clean-up job accomplished according to the moral, political and military evaluations that were represented. It was so clean, in fact, that there were blank screens assuring the protocols of propriety – the covering up of coverage – but also it was so clean on our side of the line in the sand that the American body, if it was to be lost, did so in an ascension of friendly fire. The point is that the other side never got to us, which I shall try to analyze briefly as the immunopathological dimension of this war.

For the duration of the war, contact with the negated other was nanominimalist and the language of contact was suspended. Thus, even the inevitable contaminations implied by linkage were avoided. No linkage means, among other received things, no parasitical or random eruptions on the mainline of firing, but also no complexity and no ambivalence concerning this war, its aims or the aims of man (the new order is about the aims of man, and we know which way they're aiming). The disassociation of communicating parts – no linkage – reflects the effects of derealization that the war continues to produce on us.

So: where were we? Before I say more, I want to say that I am assuming that we are still here, which is to say that I take it for granted that your opinions, evaluations and feelings concerning this war have been formed. If at this point I say that you are still with me, this is in part because the war in the Gulf has destabilized our understanding of location, and has instituted a teletopical logic: a logic of spaces aligned according to technological mappings, where the near is far and vice versa, and where systems of boundaries and borderlines will have to be entirely rethought.

If we are still here, which is not only a place but also a time of reflection – a site where geopolitical and chronopolitical tensions are being played out – this also means that we are particularly sensitized to economies of justice that the war has rendered transparent. In this area of discourse which we share, certain economies have come to light, but it is the light of apparent contradiction. I shall take one crucial example.

We constitute a community of readers and speakers who have stressed time and again that the cost of this war has drained the resources of AIDS research, or at least we have noticed that our friends with AIDS are not receiving the support they urgently require. We have wondered collectively and singly about the displacement of funds from health concerns to the demands of the military. It appears that there exists a contradiction between the external and internal needs of this country. However, this is not a contradiction, nor a blindspot, nor even a fundamental displacement of a psychic investment. The war on the Gulf is a war on AIDS. Let me explain. The lack of AIDS support and the war investment are part of the same experience of a national desire to the extent that the war has been guided by a rhetoric of renewal and regeneration, in other words, this war was conducted entirely within the symbolic registers of fascistic health. In his essay entitled ‹Our History› French philosopher Jean-Luc Nancy has argued that an ‹ideology must be called «fascist» in the general sense in which themes of spiritual and national regeneration, of the vigorous recovery of health through firmness and discipline, correspond to a fascist or fascistic vision of things›.[4] What this means basically is that in the name of symbolic health, a unity of world which sees its image in wholesomeness and the project of renewal, we have waged war on what was repeatedly represented as degenerate, sickly, something that carried the threat of contagion. In this regard, America has been carrying out its newly transcendentalized project of killing the unwell, the contaminated. The enemy is imagined as being disorderly, inefficient, tactically illiterate, dysfunctional and to a certain degree, the projected solution, cybernetics, promises to overcome such instabilities.

The hygienic project has everything to do with establishing a new world order that consists in nothing less than purifying an imaginary – and real – territory, guaranteeing that it be proper, that it espouse values of propriety und property. The invisibility of the enemy inhabits this logic, which is essentially viral. Our war body has not only tested itself, but it has come out of this test site relatively intact, clean, healthy. This accounts for the other apparent contradiction: our insensible casuality rate, their massacre. Our surgical strike, their bodies. Our high tech shoots, their blood. This was a translation, on a world-historical scale, of the AIDS test on which we scored HIV – because this was a safe war, run by the telelogic of what this panel is provisionally calling ‹virtual reality› – which is almost an anagram of viral reality. Some of you may know that virtual comes from the Latin virtus, strength, manliness. Meanwhile, back at the Gulf, we have once again instituted an autoimmune laboratory. I wish to emphasize that I am equally analyzing the symbolic effects of the war according to the letter of the war, which is to say that I take the theater of operations, the rhetoric of surgery and other health metaphors, quite seriously. I even take seriously the fact that the Bush family has its own private theater of thyroid operations, which, as if his disease had externalized itself, is called in medical terms a thyroid storm. Commander-in-chief of one storm, the President is internally dominated by another storm. This in itself suggests how difficult it is to locate the origin of the storm – inside the deserted presidential body, in the resurrection of Nazi terminology (storm troopers) or in the projections onto the desert.

On a less unconscious level of corporeal transmission, the desert has been conflated with woman's body. This brings me to my next question. Why have we stormed the figure of a woman's body, why have we entered this mysterious legacy? Given the constraints of time, I can only point to where we might go in order to explore the imaginary contours of a feminine body which our forces stormed (of course you know that before they went up, fighter pilots were fed attack doses of pornography. This, together with drugs, would help them to drop on the feminized body of Iraq while at the same time we were protecting

Kuwait from rape). If this were a seminar, and perhaps it is, I would ask you to turn your attention to Jacques Lacan's essay on ‹Aggressivity and Paranoia in Psychoanalysis› which is in *Ecrits*. Here you will find Lacan interpreting Melanie Klein's excellent work on the co-ordinates of original aggressivity. Through Melanie Klein we know the function of the imaginary primordial enclosure formed by the image of the mother's body: through her we have the cartography of the mother's internal empire, the historical atlas of the intestinal divisions in which the imagos of the fathers and brothers («real or virtual». says Lacan), in which the voracious aggression of the subject himself, dispute their deleterious (destructive) dominance over her sacred regions. What I would have to point out with regard to the particularity of this war, which may or may not be generalizable to other wars, is that the figure of the mother was always prominent, on both sides (‹the mother of all battles.› etc.), and that it was always understood that we were in a region of some originarity – the site of primordial aggression – the sacred origin of all culture. Because we were in a zone of primordial encounter, it was also read as a place of *armageddon* and apocalyptic showdown. This was the end that was also to designate a beginning: the new world order. As the original war, it encompassed all the wars in modern history: the world wars, Viet Nam, etc.

Because the war had assumed the status as origin, the initiator of the new world order, and is being conducted in the womb and cradle of our civilization, it is not at all far-fetched to read with Lacan this war in its rapport to the subject's paranoiac mapping of the maternal body. A splinter of evidence in support of this view could be retrieved from the compulsive focus on the mothers who went to war. This insistence names the symptom – the mother's body – but in the mode of disavowal. Mother may have gone to war but she was not the site of aggression: mother was finally on the map but she was not the map itself or a conflictual site constituted by the imaginary. This leads us to ask

more generally. What is the battlefield? What are its boundaries and symbolic localities? When does the battlefield take place? And how does it place us? What about the myth of the home-front? And so on. In any case, Lacan in this difficult but crucial text establishes a link between space and aggressivity, which is to say that the domination of space is related to the narcissistic fear of damage to one's own body. In fact, he argues that the fear of death, the ‹absolute Master› according to Hegel, is subordinate to the narcissistic fear of damage to one's own body. Aggressivity, as one of the intentional co-ordinates of the human ego, especially relative to the category of space and this includes real or virtual space – allows us to conceive of its role in modern neurosis. The pre-eminence of aggressivity in our civilization, Lacan adds, would be sufficiently demonstrated already by the fact that it is usually confused in ‹normal› morality with the virtue of strength. The glorification of strength as a social value is a sign of social devastation initiated on a planetary scale and justified by the image of a laissez-faire of the strongest predators. This condition should set off our psycho-alerts.
Now, as I suggested earlier I was a bit puzzled by my assignment. The connectedness between virtual reality and the war was not entirely evident to me. The promise of VR is immense, at times liberatory and very careful in its articulated negotiations with metaphysics, technology and play. I was initially perplexed because VR is something so new that it has only begun to display its existence; the war, on the other hand seemed like something that ought to have been obsolesced, and in fact it was, though it did happen and it did tend to make claims for high tech breakthroughs. This war incorporated many wars and was played out in a spectral battlefield: WWI (the gas masks) WWII (the calculated resurrection of Hitler), the Viet Nam syndrome. These phantom wars that participated in the Gulf even included the war we did not have with the Russians, or for that matter, with the Martians. Can we live without an enemy?

But if indeed there is something new about this war at a time of felt closure – most of us figured that the conditions for real war were vanishing, and that war games were a residual symptom of a history of battle – if we still feel that we are in a time of closure, then we have to recognize that closure is not the same thing as the end. Closure does not simply close a domain or an epoch: by tracing the limits of its possibilities, the closure also reaches the other side of its limit, exposing itself to its own exterior. In ‹Our History›, Nancy has shown that there is no simple opposition or interiority of the closure to the opening, and this is perhaps where VR comes into the picture.

A question that VR poses, in its full positivity, is where to locate the community. Because we are vanishing. In the absence of the polis, something like VR obligates us to pose ethical questions about contact, memory, the prosthetic subject, and it teaches us to dislocate our proper place.

There is no proper place: this includes ghettos and kitchens and all corresponding systems of the proper place. The politics of a room of one's own has to be rethought today, however enlightened it was yesterday. The question is a hard one, surpassing as it does the video game logic of good vs. evil, winner and loser, presence and absence: Can there be an atopicality of the community that nonetheless gathers, a community going nowhere, but *ecstatic*, a community of shattered egos, where the control towers come tumbling down, and where the other is genuinely anticipated? By this I also mean the other technologies.

[Support our Tropes I, was first presented at San Francisco Art Institute: Conference on Mass Media, Virtual Reality & the Persian Gulf, June 12, 1991]

NOTES

[1] See Timothy Druckrey, ‹Revenge of the Nerds›. An Interview with Jaron Lanier› in Afterimage May/1991. Some of the utterances that invite interpretation include also ‹This technology has the promise of transcending the body, depending on what you think a body is› There's no object that could be less biological or messy. It doesn't have blood, it doesn't fart, it doesn't have eczema. The slick blackness of technology is a way of avoiding the messiness of the body. I think that's why sometimes you see more men associated with this technology than women. Men find themselves in a more desperate situation with the flight from death. ‹From a political point of view the clear precedent for virtual reality is the telephone› ‹I view VR as a fancy telephone in many ways› ‹the young generation who saw the political stakes in struggles over representation ... Now they have to face up to its indetermination. Is there something like an ethics of technology?› ‹What I'm hoping the virtual reality technology will do is sensitize people to these subjective or experiential aspects of life and help them notice what a marvelous, mystical thing it is to communicate with another person.›

[2] John Barlow, ‹Life in the Data Cloud: Scratching our Eyes Back In› (Interview with Jaron Lanier) in Mondo 2000/Summer, 1990:2. ‹The computer is a map you can inhabit. Which is very seductive. It's mostly seductive because you love what you have to struggle for, but it's also seductive because it makes you seem very powerful. So it's good for the ego› ‹a way for people to get ecstatic and be with each other.› While the ego remains a problem, I do wish to signal that being-with (Mitsein), ecstatic temporality, and being-called are crucial issues in the philosophy of Martin Heidegger. Lanier is also inclined to plug the telephone: ‹My favorite story is the telephone. The telephone is a total win.› If Lanier is unwilling to count the losses, and keeps tallying technology according to egological scoreboards, this may be traceable to the fact that his mother was a victim of destructive technologies and suffered the dehumanizing effects of the Nazi camps. While I do not feel that it is necessarily appropriate in this case to psychoanalyze VR's unconscious genesis, I have tried to configure these relations – the material function, technology and the terroristic state in The Telephone Book Technology, Schizophrenia, Electric Speech (University of Nebraska Press. 1989).

[3] Ibid. p. 49. Also see Adam Heilbrun, ‹Virtual Reality. An Interview with Jaron Lanier› in Whole Earth Review, Fall/1989.

[4] Jean-Luc Nancy, ‹Our History› in diacritics, Fall/1990:20.

Avital Ronell
Unterstützt unsere Tropen II – (Oder warum es in Cyburbia viele Cowboys gibt)

Der vorliegende Beitrag ist Teil einer weiterführenden Auseinandersetzung mit dem technologisch konstellierten Staat, dem Golfkrieg und dem Prothesensubjekt. In SOT I (Support our Tropes I) ging ich auf die linguistische Verdrehung in der Aufforderung «unterstützt unsere Truppen», die eigentlich für uns eintreten sollten, ein, und darauf, wie diese Umkehrung oder dieser Chiasmus die gesamte Bevölkerung betraf. Dabei handelt es sich um einen faschistischen Kriegsbegriff, der bewußt im Sinne einer psycho-logistischen oder propagandistischen Kontrolle der Zivilbevölkerung zuhause, sozusagen der Heimatfront, vom bestehenden Zusammenhang zwischen Kriegsschauplatz und Truppenmobilisierung ablenkt. Daraus ergab sich noch eine weitere Verdrehung: Was bedeutet es, wenn das Heim für das Schauspiel des Unternehmens [Anm. des Übersetzers: Im Amerikanischen findet für Manöverplanung der sowohl medizinisch als auch dramatisch zu verstehende Begriff ‹Theater of operations› – *Operationssaal* – Anwendung] vereinnahmt wird, indem es zur Front umfunktioniert wird? In der zur Verfügung stehenden Zeit kann ich nur einige wenige aphoristische Erklärungen anbieten. Im Hinblick auf eine notwendigerweise weitere Erörterung dieser Dinge, muß ich versuchen, so klar wie möglich in der Darstellung zu bleiben, ohne der Komplexität auszuweichen, der ein derartiger Denkprozeß gerecht werden muß, um den eigenen Anspruch zu erfüllen. Krieg ist eine Belastung für uns alle: Denken begleitet die Belastung und führt zur tatsächlichen Entnervung, Beunruhigung und dem Gefühl, den Boden unter den Füßen zu verlieren. Meine Sache ist dieser zwielichtige Bereich zwischen Wissen und Unsicherheit, denn die verantwortliche Oberhand (und übrigens nicht die Ihre oder meine) hatte sich verhalten, als wüßte sie wohin es ging, und daher implizit auch, wo wir gewesen sind. Dabei geht es, unter anderem, um die *psycho-Topologien des täglichen Lebens.*

«Nun, wo waren wir?» sagt der Gelehrte. Mein Anliegen ist die Virtuelle Realität, die Medien und der Krieg am Golf. Ich glaube nicht, daß ich die Materialien, oder gar Immaterialien (Virtuelle Realität führt zur Frage der Immaterialität) beherrsche – ich meine nicht,die nötigen Fähigkeiten zu besitzen, Wissen richtig vermitteln zu können oder um Zusammenhänge aufzuzeigen. Und doch geht es hier um Fähigkeit und Beherrschung, und ich selbst halte mich für einen Infomanen. VR ist ein philosophisch komplexer Themenbereich, obgleich ein System, welches auf klassischen Tropen der Darstellung, Vorstellung, des souveränen Subjektes und der negierten Andersartigkeit aufbaut (Hegel bezeichnete die negierte Andersartigkeit als den Feind). Also hängt VR mit einer Vielzahl metaphysischer Sehnsüchte zusammen, aber wer hat diese nicht? Man sollte sich durchaus eingestehen, daß es schon immer den Wunsch, den Körper hinter sich zu lassen, gegeben hat, und ich sage oft, daß ich gern meinen eigenen Körper der Science Fiction zur Verfügung stellen würde. Aber das Überlassen des Körpers zu Lebzeiten ist Teil einer metaphysischen Sehnsucht nach einem unbestimmbaren Woanders. VR verhindert die herrschenden Verschlüsselungen dieses historischen Verlangens nach Transzendenz und Entäußerung, und sie verdient es, in all ihren Ausuferungen beachtet zu werden. Da VR auch mit dem Sein-in-der-Welt und der Befreiung des Daseinsortes vom materiellen Raum zu tun hat, ist sie auch der Versuch, Möglichkeiten des Teilhabens an der Welt neuzuordnen. Laut Jaron Lanier, Howard Rheingold und anderen, verfolgt VR eine Politik der Endlichkeit[1] und verlangt nach einer *Ethik der Technik*. Denn, während schließlich VR mittels Steckkontakt in der Mattel Corporation, dem Militär und bei der NASA Anwendung findet, ist sie gleichzeitig auch ein Hilfsmittel beim Entwerfen von Architektur und bei Versuchen in den medizinischen Wissenschaften. «Also, wo waren wir?» fragt der Gelehrte. Eine rigorose Untersuchung in vollem Umfang von VR läßt sich innerhalb des engen Rahmens dieser Erörterung nicht bewerkstelligen, aber ich möchte versuchen, einige Fragen anzuregen, die die Richtung meiner Überlegungen zu diesem schwierigen Thema darlegen.

Virtuelle Realität, künstliche Realität, Datenraum oder Cyberspace sind bezeichnend für ein Wunschdenken, dessen wichtigstes Symptom in der fehlenden Gemeinschaft zu sehen ist. In Laniers Diskurs geht es vor allem um die Möglichkeiten, eine ekstatische Gemeinschaft zu schaffen, die sich weigern würde, zielorientiert oder von einer totalitären Einheitsbestrebung regiert zu werden. Es ist, als wäre Lanier versucht, Batailles Gemeinschaft der gespaltenen Ichs heraufzubeschwören. Das metaphysische Subjekt wird zu einem gewissen Grad aufgebrochen und entlang verschiedener Wege sich aufspaltender Disidentifikation verschoben. Es kann sich dann nicht mehr in der Identifikation mit einem konkreten Bild festankern. Dennoch betont Lanier, wie alle Vermittler seitens der Radio-VR (hier wird VR eher mit einem Radio oder Telefon verglichen, unabhängig von der televisuellen Maschinerie) die Ich-verstärkende Macht der VR Entwürfe. Hinter dieser Behauptung verbirgt sich eine Zweischneidigkeit, die es mit nicht nachlassender, kritischer Schärfe zu untersuchen gilt. In Cyburbia besteht immer das Risiko, den Unterschied zwischen Simulation und ausführender Welt zu verwischen. Ich bin nicht sicher, ob dies die Entstehung einer wirklich neuen Gefahr mit sich zieht, obgleich andere das denken. Weitaus gravierender ist womöglich, daß es immer noch die Tendenz gibt, die technische Prothese nachträglich an ein metaphysisches Subjekt anzubinden, an das souveräne Subjekt der Geschichte, den Kopiloten des Schicksals. Mit anderen Worten: Die technische Prothese wäre nichts weiter als ein vom ausgeglichenen Subjekt ausgeliehenes Hilfsmittel zur Verstärkung und Intensivierung seiner selbst, ein Subjekt, dessen Fragmentierung sozusagen eine Simulation ist – d.h. ein Mittel zur *Verleugnung* der Fragmentierung, des Ich-Verlustes oder anders gesagt, der Kastration. Der Verleugnungsaspekt erst erklärt in gewisser Weise, warum Lanier es für seinen Teil vorgezogen hätte, VR mit dem, was er ausdrücklich «intentionale Realität» nennt, bezeichnet zu sehen. Dieses wirft die umfangreiche Problematik des intentionalen Bewußtseins auf, die ich an dieser Stelle kurz umreißen möchte. Das intentionale Bewußtsein ist ein philosophisches Konstrukt, welches sich ergibt, wenn der Eindruck entsteht, man hätte nicht die Kontrolle über seine Aktionen; und genau an diesem Punkt greift Laniers Projekt, in den Kontrollräumen seiner Majestät, des Ichs. Zusätzlich zur Argumentation, VR wäre «gut für das Ich», verfällt er in einen Angriff auf die Passivität des zeitgenössischen Subjektes. Jener – auf den ersten Blick durchaus verständliche – Angriff gegen die Passivität wird jedoch im zweifelhaften Namen von Tatendrang und Beherrschung geführt.[2] Das Subjekt wird die Kontrolle ergreifen. Der Standpunkt gegen die Passivität, den ich hier nur kurz berühren kann, ist, wie ich meine, hochproblematisch; obgleich auch ich mit der Notwendigkeit, radikale Kreativität zu aktivieren, übereinstimme. Aber die Gegenüberstellung von passiv und aktiv ist als Gleichung fehl am Platz. Schauen Sie sich um. Sind wir als Zivilisation nicht *zu* aktiv, *zu* tatkräftig gewesen, selbst wenn die Aktion in die Darstellung des traumatisierten Zuschauers und des manischen Kriegers zerfällt? Liebe Mädchen und Jungen – jede nicht kritisch hinterfragte Erfindung, die im Namen der

Aktion gemacht wird, muß doch unser tiefstes Mißtrauen erwecken. Eine wirkliche Ethik der Gemeinschaft, ob nun im Cyberspace oder für Liebende, Leser, Künstler, *Aktivisten und so fort müßte eine Passivität jenseits der Passivität ausfindig machen* – einen Raum des Innehaltens und der Reflexion, einen Raum, der den Anderen zum Vorschein kommen lassen würde. Sich dem Anderen oder dem Tod des Anderen auszusetzen hat nichts mit Aktionismus als solchem zu tun. Ich werde in Kürze noch darauf zurückkommen. Es ist aufgrund einer expliziten Forderung nach Taten, daß sich Cyberspace auch westlich vom Wilden Westen befindet, d.h. er ist das Memorex-Cowboy-Grenzland.

Einer der Fehler den Lanier macht, ist zu behaupten, daß «schließlich alles von Menschen gemacht ist und die Technik ist nur ein kleines Spiel, das wir spielen.»[3] Der Krieg hat gezeigt, daß die Menschen nicht nur ein kleines Spiel spielen. Weder befindet sich die Technik in einem von uns getrennten Bereich, sondern Kybernetik und künstliche Intelligenz haben gezeigt, wie Mensch-Maschinistische Hybridgebilde eine Umbildung des menschlichen Wesens mit sich bringen, welche dem Verlauf völlig neuartiger Ausrichtungen von Selbst und dem Technokörper folgt. Nun hat man seit Marvin Minsky den menschlichen Körper zur «blutigen Schweinerei organischer Materie» degradiert. Ich bin keine beharrliche Feministin, meine aber durchaus, daß diese Äußerung niemals von einer Frau, die jeden Monat eine Hypothek auf ihren Körper aufnimmt in Gestalt eines periodischen Blutbades und prämenstruellem Streß, hätte gemacht werden können. Vielleicht ist das zu forsch gesagt, aber es muß dringend erkannt werden, daß der Körper der Frau in einem fundamentalen Verhältnis zu Tod, Verzweiflung, Endlichkeit – und dem Leben steht. Während sich im weiblichen Körper die ewige Wiederkehr der «blutigen Schweinerei organischer Materie» vollzieht, übt sich der kybernetische Soldat in seinen Kommando- und Kontrollsystemen auf den Feldern der Verleugnung. Die intentionale

Realität löscht den Körper als organische, finite, verletzbare, ausnehmbare, kastrierbare und zerstörbare Einheit aus, und verschließt somit alle Körperöffnungen und verhindert Ausflüsse und Exkremente. Wir sind nicht mehr weit entfernt von der Vision Deleuzes und Guattaris eines organleeren Körpers. Verschluß der Körperausgänge und exkrementale Kontrolle helfen zu erklären, warum dieser Krieg wie besessen unter dem Zeichen der Sauberkeit geführt wurde: Im Sprachgebrauch der amerikanischen Seite war es ein sauberer Krieg, ausgeführt als Säuberungsauftrag, nach den geltenden moralischen, politischen und militärischen Regeln des Tages. Tatsächlich war der Krieg so sauber, daß die Bildschirme leer blieben, um das Protokoll des Anstands zu wahren – die Verschleierung der Entschleierung der Berichterstattung – er war außerdem auf unserer Seite der Linie im Sand derart sauber, daß der amerikanische Körper, so er fallen mußte, dieses im Kugelhagel freundlichen Feuers tat. Die Sache ist die, daß die andere Seite niemals an uns herangelangte, ich möchte versuchen, dieses kurz als die immuno-pathologische Dimension des Krieges zu analysieren.

Während der Dauer des Krieges war die Berührung mit dem verleugneten Anderen eine nanominimalistische, und Sprache, als Mittel der Kontaktaufnahme, war außer Kraft gesetzt. Somit wurde sogar der sonst unausweichlich aus den entstehenden Zusammenhängen verursachten Verseuchung entgangen. Bei dem was uns über den Bildschirm zugemutet wurde, bedeutet kein Zusammenhang entstehen zu lassen (no Linkage), daß keine parasitären oder unvorhergesehenen Schüsse auf der Hauptfeuerlinie zu sehen waren; aber auch, Komplexität in der Berichterstattung oder Ambivalenz den Krieg und dessen Ziele oder gar die vermeintlichen Interessen der gesamten Menschheit betreffend, nicht zuzulassen; (bei der Neuen Ordnung geht es um Belange der gesamten Menschheit, und wir wissen, in welche Richtung diese zielen). Die Disassoziierung von miteinander in Verbindung stehenden Teilen – keine Verbindung, kein

‹Linkage› – spiegelt die Effekte der Derealisierung wider, die dieser Krieg nach wie vor bei uns verursacht.

Also: Wo waren wir? Bevor ich mehr sage, möchte ich erwähnen, daß ich annehme, wir befinden uns noch hier. Damit ist gemeint, daß Ihre Meinungen, Einschätzungen und Gefühle hinsichtlich dieses Krieges vorgeformt worden sind. Wenn ich mich an dieser Stelle vergewissere, ob Sie noch mitkommen, dann ist das zum Teil darauf zurückzuführen, daß der Krieg am Golf unser Ortsgefühl destabilisiert und durch eine teletopische Logik ersetzt hat: Eine räumliche Logik, die sich an der technologischen Kartenzeichnung ausrichtet, wo das Nahe sich entfernt und umgekehrt und wo Grenzsysteme und Grenzverläufe völlig neu überdacht werden wollen.

Wenn wir demnach noch hier sind, womit nicht nur ein Ort, sondern auch eine Zeit der Reflexion gemeint ist – ein Ort, an dem sich sowohl geopolitische als auch chronopolitische Spannungen entladen – dann bedeutet das auch, daß wir besonders auf Ökonomien von Gerechtigkeit sensibilisiert sind, die dieser Krieg klar herausgestellt hat. In diesem Bereich der Übereinstimmung des Diskurses sind bestimmte Ökonomien ans Licht getreten, aber es ist das Licht einer offensichtlichen Widersprüchlichkeit. Ich werde ein Paradebeispiel herausgreifen.

Wir stellen eine Gemeinschaft von Lesern und Rednern dar, die immer wieder betont haben, daß dieser Krieg die Mittel, die der AIDS Forschung zur Verfügung stehen, verringert hat oder zumindest haben wir bemerkt, daß unsere Freunde mit AIDS nicht die Hilfe bekommen, die sie so dringend benötigen. Wir haben uns gemeinsam und einzeln über die Umschichtung von Mitteln aus der medizinischen Versorgung für die Erfordernisse des Militärs gewundert. Es scheint, als gäbe es einen Widerspruch zwischen den äußeren und den inneren Bedürfnissen dieses Landes. Es besteht jedoch kein Gegensatz, auch kein toter Winkel, oder eine fundamentale Verschiebung psychischer Besetzung. Der Krieg am Golf ist ein Krieg gegen AIDS: Lassen Sie mich erklären. Der mangelnde Einsatz gegen

AIDS und die Anstrengungen im Krieg gehören insofern zur selben Erfahrung eines nationalen Bedürfnisses, als daß der Krieg von einer Rhetorik der Erneuerung und Regeneration bestimmt war; mit anderen Worten, dieser Krieg wurde ganz innerhalb der symbolischen Register faschistischer Gesundheitsideale geführt. In seinem Aufsatz ‹Unsere Geschichte› vertritt der französische Philosoph Jean-Luc Nancy die Meinung, daß eine ‹Ideologie als allgemein «faschistisch» bezeichnet werden muß, wenn in ihr Themen spiritueller und nationaler Erneuerung und der Erlangung kraftstrotzender körperlicher Gesundheit durch Strenge und Disziplin im Zusammenhang mit einer faschistoiden oder faschistischen Vision der Dinge zum Tragen kommen.[4]› Im Grunde heißt das nichts anderes, als daß wir im Namen einer Gesundheitssymbolik, einer einheitlichen Welt, die als ihr Abbild strotzende Gesundheit und ein Vorhaben der Erneuerung sieht, einen Krieg gegen alles, was wiederholt als entartet, kränkelnd und bedrohlich ansteckend dargestellt wurde, geführt haben. Amerika führt in dieser Beziehung sein neuerdings transzendentalisiertes Vorhaben einer Eliminierung des Ungesunden und Verseuchten aus. Der Gegner wird als undiszipliniert, ineffizient, taktisch unfähig und nicht zweckmäßig dargestellt, und in gewisser Weise verspricht die vorgeschlagene Lösung, nämlich die Kybernetik, derartig unberechenbare Faktoren zu überwinden.

Dieses hygienische Projekt hat ausschließlich die Begründung einer neuen Weltordnung zum Ziel, die aus nichts weniger als der Säuberung eines imaginären – und realen – Territoriums entsteht, aus der Gewährleistung einer dortigen Ordnung und der Achtung der Werte von Sitte, Anstand und Eigentum. Diese Logik geht von der Unsichtbarkeit des Feindes aus, d.h. wir haben es im Grunde mit einer Virus-Logik zu tun. Unser Kriegskörper hat sich nicht nur selbst getestet, sondern er ist relativ intakt, sauber und gesund vom Testgelände gekommen. Hier findet sich die Erklärung für den anderen vermeintlichen Widerspruch: zwischen unserer eigenen, nicht erfaßbaren

Todesrate und dem Massaker des Gegners; unser chirurgisch genauer Angriff, ihre Leichen; unsere Schüsse aus hochtechnologischen Waffen, ihr Blut. Es war die Übertragung des AIDS-Tests auf welthistorischen Maßstab, wobei wir im Ergebnis als HIV-negativ herauskamen, denn dieser Krieg war ja sicher, er vollzog sich nach der Telelogik dessen, was die hier Anwesenden provisorisch «virtuelle Realität» nennen – übrigens beinahe ein Anagramm von Virus-Realität. Einigen unter Ihnen mag bekannt sein, daß sich virtuell aus dem Lateinischen *Virtus* für Stärke, Männlichkeit, ableitet. Zurück an den Golf. Hier haben wir wieder einmal ein Immunforschungslabor eingerichtet. Ich möchte betonen, daß ich mich ebenso mit den *symbolischen Auswirkungen des Krieges* nach allen Regeln des Kriegsrechts auseinandersetze, d. h. ich nehme das Beispiel des Manöverfelds als Operationsraum, die Rhetorik aus der Chirurgie und die Verwendung anderer medizinischer Metaphern sehr ernst. Ich berücksichtige sogar die Tatsache, daß sich in der Familie Bush das private Schauspiel mehrerer Schilddrüsenoperationen abspielte, was im medizinischen Fachjargon als Schilddrüsensturm bezeichnet wird. Als Oberkommandierender eines Sturms wird der Präsident innerlich von einem ganz anderen Sturm bedrängt. Jetzt zeigt sich, wie schwierig es ist, den Ausgangspunkt des Sturms zu lokalisieren, ob im verwüsteten Körper des Präsidenten, oder im neuerlichen Auferwachen Nationalsozialistischer Begrifflichkeiten (Sturmtruppen), oder in den Wüstenprojektionen auf dem Bildschirm.

Auf einem weniger unbewußten Niveau korporealer Vermittlung ist der weibliche Körper immer wieder mit der Wüste verglichen worden. Das führt mich zu meiner nächsten Frage. Warum mußten wir das Sinnbild eines weiblichen Körpers erstürmen, warum taucht hier dieses mysteriöse Erbe auf? In der kurzen Zeit kann ich nur Vermutungen anstellen, in welcher Richtung wir uns bewegen müßten, um die imaginären Umrisse des weiblichen Körpers zu erforschen, den unsere Truppen stürmten (Sie wissen natürlich, daß den Kampfpiloten zur Steigerung der Angriffslust vor dem Start eine Dosis Pornographie verabreicht wurde. Zusammen mit Medikamenten erleichterte es ihnen die Bombadierung des weiblich besetzten irakischen Körpers, während sie zur gleichen Zeit Kuwait vor weiterer Vergewaltigung schützten). Wäre dies ein Seminar – vielleicht ist es ja eines – so würde ich Ihre Aufmerksamkeit auf Lacans Aufsatz über ‹Aggressivität und Paranoia in der Psychoanalyse› lenken, welcher in den *Ecrits* zu finden ist. Dort interpretiert er Melanie Kleins hervorragende Arbeit über die Koordinaten ursprünglicher Aggression. Von Melanie Klein kennen wir die Funktion des imaginären Urgeheges, das aus der *Vorstellung* des mütterlichen Körpers entstanden ist: von der Mutter erhalten wir eine Kartographie über ihr Innenleben, den historischen Atlas ihrer Darmabschnitte, in denen die Vorstellungen der Väter und Brüder («sowohl real als auch virtuell», sagt Lacan) und das aggressionshungrige Subjekt selbst sich gegenseitig die auslöschende (und zerstörerische) Herrschaft über ihre heiligen Regionen streitig machen. Besonders im Zusammenhang mit der Einmaligkeit dieses Krieges möchte ich darauf aufmerksam machen – vielleicht mit anderen Kriegen vergleichbar, oder auch nicht – nämlich, daß die Figur der Mutter auf beiden Seiten immer wieder deutlich und betont in den Vordergrund gerückt wurde (‹die Mutter aller Gefechte› usw.). Es war auch die ganze Zeit klar, daß wir uns in einem geographischen Gebiet von gewisser historischer Bedeutung für die Entstehungsgeschichte der Menschheit befanden – der Ort der Uraggression – der heilige Ursprung der gesamten Kultur. Weil wir es mit einer Zone der Urbegegnung zu tun hatten, konnte diese auch als Schauplatz für Armageddon und eine apokalyptisch beispielhafte Machtprobe gelesen werden. Es war das Ende, welches auch einen Neubeginn signalisieren sollte: Eine neue Weltordnung. Als originaler Krieg verkörperte er alle Kriege der Neuzeit, die Weltkriege, Vietnam, usw..

Da der Krieg den Status einer Entstehungsgeschichte angenommen hatte und als Initiator für eine neue Weltordnung galt, und da er sich in der Gebärmutter und Wiege der Menschheit abspielte, ist es keineswegs abwegig, mit Lacan den Krieg in seinem Verhältnis mit dem Subjekt und dessen paranoider Zeichnung des mütterlichen Körpers zu lesen. Ein Beweissplitter zur Unterstützung dieser Ansicht könnte sich aus der zwanghaften Aufmerksamkeit herleiten, die den Müttern, die in den Krieg zogen, gewidmet wurde. Die Beharrlichkeit gibt dem Symptom einen Namen – Mutters Körper, aber ausgesprochen wird er wie eine Verleugnung. Mutter mag in den Krieg gezogen sein, war aber selbst nicht der Austragungsort von Aggressionen: Mutter erschien endlich auf der Landkarte, aber sie war nicht die Karte selbst oder gar konfliktbeladener Ort, der sich aus dem Imaginären konstituiert. So müssen wir viel allgemeiner fragen: Was ist das Schlachtfeld? Wo sind seine Grenzen und symbolischen Lokalitäten? Wann entsteht ein Schlachtfeld? Und wo befinden wir uns im Verhältnis dazu? Was ist mit dem Mythos Heimfront? Und so fort ... Auf jeden Fall entdeckt Lacan in diesem wichtigen Text einen Zusammenhang zwischen Raum und Aggressivität, soll meinen, daß die Vorherrschaft im Raum im Zusammenhang mit der narzißtischen Angst vor der Beschädigung des eigenen Körpers steht. Er meint sogar, daß die Angst vor dem Tod, dem «absoluten Herr» Hegels, der narzißtischen Angst vor der Verletzung des eigenen Körpers untergeordnet ist. Die Aggressivität als eine der bewußten Koordinaten des menschlichen Ichs, besonders im Verhältnis zur Kategorie Raum – das schließt realen oder virtuellen Raum ein – läßt uns nachdenklich über deren Bedeutung für die Neurose der Moderne werden. Die Vorherrschaft der Aggressivität in unserer Kultur, so fährt Lacan fort, ergibt sich allein schon aus der Tatsache, daß sie herkömmlicherweise unter ‹normalen› Moralitätsbegriffen mit der Tugend der Stärke verwechselt wird. Die Glorifizierung der Stärke als gesellschaftlicher Wert ist ein Anzeichen der sozialen Zerstörung, die in globalem Ausmaß um sich gegriffen hat und welcher durch Sinnbilder des Laisser-Faire für die jeweils stärksten Plünderer stattgegeben wird. Dieser Zustand sollte unsere psycho-alerten Experten in Bewegung setzen.

Nun, wie ich schon vorhin anmerkte, stand ich etwas verwirrt vor der sich mir stellenden Aufgabe. Der Zusammenhang zwischen virtueller Realität und Krieg war mir nicht ganz klar. Die Möglichkeiten von VR können immens, manchmal befreiend und äußerst differenziert in der Vermittlung zwischen Metaphysik, Technik und Spiel sein. Auch war ich anfänglich so perplex, weil VR etwas derart Neues ist, daß ihre Existenz gerade erst sichtbar geworden ist; Krieg hingegen schien wie etwas, das längst hätte obsolet sein sollen, und er war es auch. Dennoch fand er statt und stellte sich in der Tendenz so dar, als wären in ihm hochtechnologische Neuerungen zum Durchbruch gelangt. Dieser Krieg barg viele Kriege in sich, den 1. Weltkrieg (Gasmasken), den 2. Weltkrieg (in der kalkulierten Wiederbelebung einer Hitlerfigur), das Vietnam Syndrom; und er wurde auf einem spektralen Schlachtfeld geführt. Diese Phantomkriege, die beim Golfkrieg mitwirkten, schließen auch den Krieg, den wir nicht mit den Russen – oder gar mit den Marsmenschen – geführt haben, ein. Können wir ohne einen Feind bestehen?

Wenn es tatsächlich etwas Neues an diesem Krieg unter dem Eindruck einer Endzeit gibt – die meisten von uns glaubten, die Bedingungen für einen wirklichen Krieg wären nahezu verschwunden und Kriegsspiele nur der symptomatische Überrest einer Geschichte voller Schlachten – und wenn wir immer noch denken, wir sind in einer Endzeit, dann müssen wir erkennen, daß Endzeit nicht das gleiche wie das Ende ist. Ein Schluß schließt nicht nur eine Domäne oder Epoche ab; indem er die Grenzen deren Möglichkeiten abzeichnet, deutet der Schluß auch über die andere Seite dieser Grenze hinweg und entblößt sich vor seinem eigenen Äußeren. Nancy hat in ‹Unsere Geschichte› gezeigt, daß es so etwas wie den einfachen Gegensatz oder Interiorität des Schlusses im Verhältnis zur Eröffnung nicht gibt; und vielleicht ist dies der Punkt, wo VR ins Bild kommt.

Eine Frage, die VR, positiv gesehen, stellt, ist nach dem Standort der Gemeinschaft – weil wir selbst dabei sind, zu verschwinden. Wenn die Polis fehlt, zwingt uns etwas wie VR ethische Fragen über Berührung, Erinnerungsvermögen und das Prothesensubjekt zu stellen, und sie lehrt uns, den angestammten Ort zu entwurzeln.

Den angestammten Ort gibt es nicht: dazu gehören die Ghettos, Küchen und alle anderen entsprechenden Systeme eines angestammten Platzes. Heute muß die Politik eines Zimmers für sich allein neu überdacht werden, so fortschrittlich sie auch gestern gewesen sein mag. Das ist eine schwierige Aufgabe, setzt sie sich doch über die einfache Videospiellogik von Gut gegen Böse, Gewinner und Verlierer, An- und Abwesenheit hinweg: Kann es eine Unaktualität der Gemeinschaft geben, die trotzdem versammelt, eine Gemeinschaft welche sich – dennoch ekstatisch – nirgendwohin bewegt, eine Gemeinschaft der vielen zerbrochenen Ichs, die die Kontrolltürme zusammenbrechen läßt und wo der Andere in wirklicher freudiger Erwartung zugelassen wird? Damit meine ich auch andere Technologien.

Aus dem Amerikanischen übersetzt von Jörg von Stein.

[Der Vortrag ‹Unterstützt unsere Tropen I wurde zuerst am 12. Juni 1991, anläßlich der Konferenz ‹Massenmedien, Virtuelle Realität und der Persische Golf› am San Francisco Art Institute gehalten]

ANMERKUNGEN

1 Siehe Timothy Druckrey: ‹Revenge of the Nerds: An Interview with Jaron Lanier.› (Die Rache der Schwachköpfe) in: Afterimage, Mai 1991. Einige der Äußerungen, die es wert wären, überprüft zu werden, lauten: «Diese Technik birgt das Versprechen der Möglichkeit, den Körper zu verlassen, je nachdem, was man für den Körper hält.» «Es gibt kein Ding, das weniger biologisch oder

dreckig sein könnte. Es hat kein Blut, furzt nicht, bekommt kein Ekzem. Das glatt elegante Schwarz der Technik bietet eine Möglichkeit, dem Schmutz des Körpers zu entgehen. Ich glaube, das ist auch einer der Gründe, warum man mehr Männer als Frauen findet, die sich mit dieser Technik beschäftigen. Männer sind in ihrer Flucht vor dem Tode in einer verzweifelteren Situation.» «Aus politischer Sicht ist das Telefon der eindeutige Vorläufer der Virtuellen Realität.» «In vieler Hinsicht sehe ich VR als ein hochentwickeltes Telefon.» «... die junge Generation, die ihr politisches Glück in Auseinandersetzungen um das Recht auf Vertretung suchte ... jetzt, wo sie auf deren Unberechenbarkeit stoßen, gibt es wenigstens so etwas wie eine Ethik der Technik?» «Was ich mir von der Virtuellen Realität erhoffe ist, daß sie die Menschen sensibler macht für diese subjektiven und unmittelbaren Erfahrungswerte des Lebens und ihnen hilft, zu bemerken, was für eine wunderbare und mystische Sache es ist, mit einer anderen Person zu kommunizieren.»

[2] John Barlow: ‹Life in the Data Cloud: Scratching Your Eyes Back In› (Ein Leben auf der Datenwolke: Wie man sich das Auge wieder einkratzt) Interview mit Jaron Lanier in: Mondo 2000, Sommer 1990, 2 ‹Der Computer ist eine Landkarte, in der man leben kann, was sehr verführerisch ist. Vor allem ist es verführerisch, weil man das liebt, wofür man kämpfen muß, aber es ist auch verführerisch, weil es einen mächtig erscheinen läßt. So ist es auch gut für das Ego.› ‹... eine Möglichkeit für die Menschen, ekstatisch zu werden und zusammen zu sein.› Während das Ich ein Problem bleibt, möchte ich darauf hinweisen, daß beisammensein *(Mitsein)*, ekstatische Zeitlichkeit, und angesprochen werden wichtige Begriffe aus Heideggers Philosophie sind. Lanier liebt es auch, sich ans Telefon zu hängen: «Meine Lieblingsgeschichte ist das Telefon. Das Telefon ist ein totaler Gewinner.» Wenn Lanier es ablehnt, die Verluste zu zählen, und aus ökologischen Gründen immer wieder die Technik bejahend Buch führt, dann *mag* das darauf zurückzu führen sein, daß seine eigene Mutter das Opfer zerstörerischer Technologien wurde, sie war Opfer der unmenschlichen Auswirkungen der Nazi Konzentrationslager. In diesem speziellen Fall glaube ich zwar nicht, daß es passend ist, die Entstehungsgeschichte des Unbewußten bei VR zu psychoanalysieren. Ich habe aber versucht, diese Zusammenhänge – das Verhältnis mütterliche Funktion, Technik und der terroristische Staat – in ‹The Telephone Book: Technology, Schizophrenia, Electric Speech› (Das Telefonbuch: Technik, Schizophrenie und elektrische Sprache) aufzuzeigen. (University of Nebraska Press, 1989)

[3] Ibid, S.49. Siehe auch Adam Heilbrun: Virtual Reality: ‹An Interview with Jaron Lanier› in: Whole Earth Review, Fall (Herbst) 1989.

[4] Jean Luc Nancy: ‹Our History› (unsere Geschichte) in: diacritics, Herbst 1990. 20.

Otto E. Rössler
Das durchsichtige Medium

Medien sind ihrem Wesen nach opak – sie entziehen sich immer dem, der sie benutzt oder von ihnen benutzt wird. Das alte Gesetz von Tschuang-Tse, daß der Fisch das Wasser am wenigsten kennt, gewinnt im Zeitalter der elektronischen Medien neue Aktualität.

Das Endo-Gefängnis der Welt ist am schwersten erkennbar. Gödel zeigte, daß nicht sämtliche Theoreme der Mathematik angegeben werden können von der Mathematik, das heißt, vom Inneren des betreffenden Systems aus. Descartes hatte zuvor erkannt, daß die ganze Welt der Erscheinungen ein Gefängnis darstellt, aus dem ein Ausweg nur möglich ist, wenn man es mathematisch konsistent beschreiben kann. Denn dann kann man die Exo/Endo-Problematik im Modell reproduzieren und verstehen, wie dies später Gödel gelang. Die Tradition von Descartes und Gödel ist die Sprengung des Gefängnisses dadurch, daß man seine Wände berührbar macht.

Philosophie und Wissenschaft erlauben ‹nur› eine Berührung mit dem Geist (‹to touch it with the mind›). Heute wird aus diesem Gedankenspiel Ernst. Die ‹elektronischen Medien› leiten eine neue Emanzipation ein, da jeder jede Information in der von ihm gewünschten Präsentation und Härte abrufen kann. Dazuhin kann er interaktiv hineingehen in die neue elektronische Bibliothek der Welt und interaktiv neue Hebel ausprobieren. Die Virtualität wird real.

Die neue ‹Flüssigkeit› ist das Kennzeichen, daß wirklich ein neues Medium vorliegt. Die neue Bewegungsfreiheit ruft uralte

Erinnerungen wach. Das neue Medium ist wie ein Spiegel: es zeigt uns ungeschützt. Wir sind immer noch kleine Kinder, die krabbeln lernen müssen auf einem fremden Fußboden.

Wo ist der Fußboden? Die Antwort ist nach wie vor, daß es niemand von uns weiß. Die alte Erkenntnis aus frühen Kindheitstagen, daß wir die Hingeworfenheit noch nachzittern spüren, als Schwere und Sklavenangst, versuchen wir meist ganz schnell zu vergessen. Für diese Flucht bieten die elektronischen Medien besonders leicht zu benutzende Wege. Die Vielkanal-Fernbedienung und der Datenhandschuh machen es möglich. Aber – und hier liegt ein kleines Wunder der Paradoxie vor – durch die neue Leichtigkeit können wir es uns leisten, ein bißchen mutiger nachzufragen als vorher, wo die Glieder noch mit Beinmuskeln statt mit bloßen Intentionsbewegungen der Finger oder des Kopfes bewegt werden mußten. Die neue Chance besteht darin, nicht nur ein Medium kennenzulernen, sondern alle Medien neu zu erkennen als eine wesentliche Struktur. Auch die Medien, die noch längst nicht an der Reihe sind in unserer Zeit, wie die eigene Körperlichkeit und Zeitlichkeit und der Tod, werden plötzlich neu ansprechbar, da die blindmachende Gewöhnung noch nicht eingesetzt hat.

Ein viertes Gefängnis ist das der Farbe. Die Farbe ist beinahe das Fremdeste, weil ihre Fremdheit von fast niemandem wahrgenommen wird. Helmholtz saß als Kind gerne auf den Knien des Vaters, wenn dieser von seinen Gesprächen mit Fichte erzählte, und gelangte so zu der Erkenntnis: ‹Alle Farben sind Falschfarben›. Wenn heute eine Voyager-Sonde bei ihrem Vorbeiflug an einem Planeten-Mond nur kleine Reflexionsunterschiede auf der Oberfläche desselben registriert, und noch dazu nur in einem ganz engen Teilfenster des sichtbaren Spektrums, dann wird später bei der Wiedergabe einfach die Verteilung der Intensitäten in diesem Fenster sowohl ‹vertikal› vergrößert (damit unser Auge die vorhandenen Unterschiede auch wirklich wahrnehmen kann), als auch ‹horizontal› auseinandergezogen auf die volle Breite des gesamten uns verfügbaren Spektrums. Das resultierende farbenprächtige Bild heißt dann ‹Falschfarbendarstellung›.

Wir sind das gewohnt und freuen uns daran. Was Helmholtz auffiel, war die Gefängnisseite dieser Medaille. Wieso gibt es eine ‹rote Welt›? Die Wissenschaft, die nur die Relationen in unserer Welt abbilden kann, wie Max Born betonte, kann weder sagen, wo Rotheit herkommt, noch, was sie ist, noch, ob sie existiert. Da die Wissenschaft im Hades – einer Schattenwelt – identisch mit der unseren wäre, müßte sie eigentlich den Beweis akzeptieren, der im Hades möglich ist: Farben existieren nicht. Irgendwo in unserem Gehirn haben wir eine ‹Kontaktmatte›, wo, wenn wir darauftreten aus Versehen (oder die Welt daraufdrückt), wir plötzlich im ‹roten Salon› sind, im roten Welt-Modus.

Ähnlich steht es mit dem Jetzt. Morgen kann der Schmerz wieder da sein, oder die Erinnerung an den Freund. Irgendetwas stimmt nicht mit der sauberen, farbigen, durchkonstruierten, jetzt so selbstverständlich erscheinenden Welt. Es gibt eine Schicht dahinter, mit ihren eigenen Sensoren, aber sie ist verdeckt. Der kleine Metalldeckel über diesen Knöpfen des großen Videorecorders unserer Welt ist normalerweise geschlossen.

Die Kunst öffnet den Deckel. Es ist Kunst, zu zeigen, daß die Welt künstlich ist. In die Kunstwelt einzugreifen und ihr das Geheimnis zu entreißen, ist die neue, durch die elektronischen Medien eröffnete Möglichkeit.

«Sieh nur, wie die Fische sich freuen im Wasser», sagte Zhouang Zhou. «Ich mag dieses Wasser; es ist eine ganz neue Freude zu schwimmen, wenn man dabei des Wassers gewahr wird», fügte er fast unhörbar hinzu. Heute können wir diesen Satz hören. Das Wort Wasser ist nur eine Metapher, ebenso das Wort Medium. Die ‹Matrix der Welt› wird hinter dem Schein sichtbar. Sie ist rot und blau und grün und vibriert.

Otto E. Rössler
The Transparent Medium

Media are in essence opaque: they recede in face of the one who uses them or is used by them. In this era of electronic media Chuang-tzu's oldest precept – that it is the fish who know the least about water – gets an update.
The endo-prison of the world is the most diffcult to perceive. Gödel demonstrates that not all mathematical theories can be defined mathematically, i.e. from inside the relevant system. Descartes had, before him, realized that the whole world of appearances represents a prison out of which the only escape possible is by a mathematically consistent description. This way you can reproduce and understand the exo/endo problem as a model, which Gödel later succeeded in demonstrating. The tradition according to Descartes and Gödel is that you break out of this prison by making the walls tangible.
Philosophy and science permit ‹only› the mind to do the touching. Today such mind games have become serious business. ‹Electronic media› are introducing a new emancipation: anyone can call up any information – in the desired form that presentation and precision demands. To do so, he need but enter the new two-way electronic world library and interactively press new levers. Virtuality becomes real.
This new ‹fluidity› is the sign that a really new medium is at hand. And this new freedom of movement calls up age-old memories. The new medium is like a mirror: it shows us defenceless. We are still little children needing to learn how to toddle on a new floor.

Where is the floor? The answer as always is: nobody knows. The memory of our childhood falls still reverberating in the apprehension of our own ponderousness and our fear of slavery is something we try to forget as quickly as possible. For this escape the electronic media offer particularly easy to use means. The multi channel remote control and the fitted data glove make it all possible. But – and herein lies a small paradoxical wonder – by means of this new lightness, we can now afford to pose questions somewhat more courageously than we used to when our limbs had to be moved by our leg muscles instead of with the mere intentioned flick of the finger or brain. The new opportunity offered is to know not just one medium, but to now appreciate all media as one essential structure. Then too, the media whose time is far from ripe – like our own corporeality and temporality, and death – can now suddenly be addressed, since blind habit has not yet set in.

A fourth prison is that of color. Color is almost the strangest of all, because its strange nature goes practically unrecognized. As a child, Helmholtz, used to like sitting on his father's lap and listen to him recounting his conversations with Fichte; it is thus that he came to the conclusion: ‹All colors are false colors.› When today a Voyager space probe flies past a planet's moon and registers only small reflection differences on its surface and that only within the narrowest partial window of the visible spectrum, these are later reproduced simply by enlarging ‹vertically› the distribution of the light intensities in this window (so that our eye can actually perceive the given differences), as well as ‹horizontally› widening them to the full band of the spectrum available to us. The resulting brightly colored image is then called ‹mock-color imaging›.

We are used to, and delight in, it. What Helmholtz had noticed was the imprisoning side of this coin. Why is there such a thing as a ‹red world›? Science, which can only reflect the given relationships within our world, as Max Born insisted, cannot say where red comes from, nor what it is, nor if indeed it exists. A science situated in Hades – a world of shade – would be identical to our own and would in fact have to accept the proof that in Hades color does not exist. Somewhere in our brain we have a ‹contact mat›, where, should we step on it by chance, we may suddenly find ourselves in a ‹red room›, in the red world mode.

It is the same with the Now. Tomorrow the pain can return or the memory of a friend. Something or other is wrong with the clean, colorful, well-constructed, so-matter-of-course apparition of the world. There is a layer behind it, with its own sensors, but it remains concealed. The small metal lid that covers the buttons of the large video-recorder/world is normally shut.

Art opens this lid. It is art to show that the world is artificial. To penetrate this artificial world and wrest its secret from it – that is the new possibility that the electronic media offer.

«Only see how happy the fish are in the water». Chuang-tzu said. «I like this water: it is an entirely new pleasure to swim when you are aware of the water.» he added almost inaudibly.

Today we have ears to hear this sentence. The word water is only a metaphor, like the word medium. The ‹matrix of the world› is becoming visible behind its apparition. It is red and blue and green and vibrates.

Slavoj Žižek
From Virtual Reality to the Virtualization of Reality

How are we to approach ‹virtual reality› from the psychoanalytical perspective? Let us take as our starting point Freud's most famous dream, that of Irma's injection[1]; the first part of the dream, Freud's dialogue with Irma, this exemplary case of a dual, specular relationship, culminates in a look into her open mouth:

«There's a horrendous discovery here, that of the flesh one never sees, the foundation of things, the other side of the head, of the face, the secretory glands par excellence, the flesh from which everything exudes, at the very heart of the mystery, the flesh in as much as it is suffering, is formless, in as much as its form in itself is something which provokes anxiety. Spectre of anxiety, identification of anxiety, the final revelation of you are this – You are this, which is so far from you, this which is the ultimate formlessness.»[2]

Suddenly, this horror changes miraculously into «a sort of ataraxia» defined by Lacan precisely as «the coming into operation of the symbolic function»[3] exemplified by the production of the formula of trimethylamin, the subject floats freely in symbolic bliss. – The trap to be avoided here, of course, is to contrast this symbolic bliss with the ‹hard reality›: the fundamental thesis of Lacanian psychoanalysis is, on the contrary, that what we call ‹reality› constitutes itself against the background of such a ‹bliss›, i.e. of such an exclusion of some traumatic Real (epitomized here by a *woman's* throat). This is precisely what Lacan has in mind when he says that fantasy is the ultimate support of reality: ‹reality› stabilizes itself when some fantasy-frame of a ‹symbolic bliss› forecloses the view into the abyss of the Real. Far from being a kind of figment of our dreams that prevents us from ‹seeing reality as it effectively is›, fantasy is constitutive of what we call reality: the most common bodily ‹reality› is constituted via a detour through the maze of imagination. In other words, the price we pay for our access to ‹reality› is that something – the reality of the trauma – must be ‹repressed›.

What strikes you here is the parallel between the dream of Irma's injection and another famous Freudian dream, that of the dead son who appears to his father and addresses him with the reproach «Father, can't you see that I'm burning?». In his interpretation of the dream of Irma's injection, Lacan draws our attention to the appropriate remark by Eric Ericson that after the look into Irma's throat, after his encounter of the Real, *Freud should have awakened* – like the dreamer of the dream of the burning son who wakes up when he encounters this horrifying apparition: when confronted with the Real in all its unbearable horror, the dreamer wakes up, i.e. escapes into ‹reality›. One has to draw a radical conclusion from this parallel between the two dreams: what we call ‹reality› is constituted exactly upon the model of the asinine ‹symbolic bliss› that enables Freud to continue to sleep after the horrifying look into Irma's throat. The anonymous dreamer who awakens into reality in order to avoid the traumatic Real of the burning son's reproach proceeds the same way as Freud who, after the look into Irma's throat, ‹changes the register›, i.e. escapes into the fantasy which veils the Real. – What has this to do with the computer? As early as 1954 Lacan pointed out that in today's world, the world of the machine proper, the paradigmatic case for ‹symbolic bliss› is the computer[4], as one can ascertain when one enacts a kind of phenomenological investigation, leaving aside (technological) questions of how the computer works, and confining oneself to its

symbolic impact, to how the computer inscribes itself into our symbolic universe.
In other words, one must conceive the computer as a ‹machine à penser› (a thinking machine) that in the sense Levi-Strauss talks about food as an ‹objet à penser› (to think about) and not just an ‹objet à manger› (to eat): because of its ‹incomprehensibility›, its almost uncanny nature, the computer is an ‹evocatory object›[5], an object which, beyond its instrumental function, raises a whole series of basic questions about the specificity of human thought, about the differences between animate and inanimate, etc. – no wonder that the computer metaphor is reproduced in miscellaneous fields and achieves universal range (we ‹program› our activities, we do away with a deadlock via ‹debugging›, etc). The computer is a third, new stage in Marx's scheme of development, which goes from tool (an extension of the human body) to machine (which works automatically and imposes its rhythm to man): on the one hand, it is closer to a tool in that it does not work automatically, man provides the rhythm etc., on the other hand it is more independently active than a machine, since it works as a partner in a dialogue in which it raises questions itself, etc. In contrast to a mechanical machine, its internal action is ‹nontransparent›, *stricto sensu* irrepresentable (we can't ‹illustrate› its working, as with a clutch or a gear box), and it operates on the basis of a dialogue with the user; for that reason, it triggers in the subject-user a split of the type ‹I know, but nevertheless ... ›: of course we know that it is ‹inanimate›, that it is only a machine, nevertheless in practice we act towards it as if it were living and thinking ...
How then does one ‹think with a computer› beyond its instrumental use? A computer is not unequivocal in its socio-symbolic effect but operates as some kind of ‹projective test›, a fantasy screen on which is projected the field of miscellaneous social reactions. Two of the main reactions are ‹Orwellian› (the computer as an incarnation of Big Brother, an example of centralized totalitarian control) and ‹anarchistic›, which in contrast sees in the

computer the possibility for a new self-managing society, ‹a co-operative of knowledge› which will enable anyone to control ‹from below› and thus make social life transparent and controllable. The common axis of this contrast is the computer as a means of control and mastery, except that in one case it is control ‹from above› and in the other ‹from below›; on the level of individual impact, this experience of the computer as a medium of mastery and control (the computer universe as a transparent, organized and controlled universe in contrast to ‹irrational› social life) is countered by an effect of wonderment and magic: when we successfully produce an intricate effect with simple program means, this creates in the observer – who of course in the final analysis is identical to the user himself – the impression that the achieved effect is out of proportion to the modest means, the impression of a hiatus between means and effect. It is of particular interest how on the level of programming itself, this opposition repeats the male/female difference in the form of the difference between ‹hard› (obsessional) and ‹soft› (hysterical) programming – the first aims at complete control and mastery, transparency, analytical dismemberment of the whole into parts; the second proceeds intuitively, it improvises, it works by trial and thus uncovers the new, it leaves the result itself ‹to amaze›, its relations to the object are more of ‹dialogue› ...
The computer works most effectively of course as an ‹evocatory object› in the question of ‹artificial intelligence› – here, an inversion has already taken place which is the fate of every successful metaphor: one first tries to simulate human thought as far as possible with the computer, bringing the model as close as possible to the human ‹original›, until at a certain point matters reverse and it raises the question: *what if this ‹model› is already a model of the ‹original› itself*, what if human intelligence itself operates like a computer, is ‹programmed›, etc.? The computer raises in pure form the question of semblance, a discourse which would not be a simulacrum: it is clear that the computer in some sense only ‹simulates› thought; *yet how does the total simulation*

of thought differ from ‹real› thought? No wonder, then, that the spectre of ‹artificial intelligence› summons the paradoxes of the prohibition of incest – ‹artificial intelligence› appears as an entity which is simultaneously prohibited and considered impossible: one asserts that it is not possible for a machine to think, at the same time being occupied in prohibiting research in these directions, on the grounds that it is dangerous, ethically dubious, etc.

The usual objection to ‹artificial intelligence› is that in the final analysis, the computer is only ‹programmed›, that it cannot in a real sense ‹understand›, while man's activities are spontaneous and creative. The first answer of the advocates of ‹artificial intelligence›: are not man's ‹creativity›, ‹spontaneity›, ‹unpredictibility› etc., an appearance which is created by the simultaneous activity of a number of programs? So the path towards ‹artificial intelligence› leads *via* the construction of a system with multiple processors ... But the main answer of advocates of ‹artificial intelligence› is above all that the computer is far from obeying a simple linear-mechanical logic: its logic follows ‹Gödel's›, the logic of self-reference, recursive functions, paradoxes, where the whole is its own part, self-applicable, etc. The idea of a computer as a closed consistent, linear machine is a mechanical, ‹pre-computer age› concept: the computer is an inconsistent machine which, caught in a snare of self-reference, can never be totalized. Here the proponents of the ‹computer culture› seek the link between science and art: in the principled, not just empirical non-totality and inconsistency of the computer – is not such self-reflective activity of the computer homologous to a Bach fugue which constantly takes up the same theme?[6]

These ideas form the basis of the hacker subculture. Hackers operate as a circle of initiates who exclude themselves from everyday ‹normality› in order to devote themselves to programming as an end in itself; their enemy is the ‹normal›, bureaucratic, instrumental, consistent, totalizing use of the computer, which does not take into account its ‹aesthetic dimension›; their ‹master-signifier›, their manna, the aim, trick, of the ‹hack› is when one succeeds in ‹beating the system› (for example, when one breaks into a protected, closed circuit of information). The hacker consequently attacks the System at the point of its inconsistency – to perform a ‹hack› means to know how to exploit the fault, the symptom of the System. The universalized metaphorical range of the ‹hack› corresponds exactly to this dimension: so, for example, in the subculture of the hacker, Gödel's theorem is understood as ‹Gödel's hack› that subverted the totalitarian logic of the Russell-Whitehead system ...

Yet in contrast to this search for the point of inconsistency of the System, the hacker's aesthetic is the aesthetic of a ‹regulated universe›. It is a universe which excludes intersubjectivity, a relation to the other *qua* subject: notwithstanding all the danger, tension, amazement which we experience when immersed in a video game, there is a basic difference between that tension and the tension in our relation to the ‹real world› – a difference which is not that the computer-generated video world is ‹just a game›, a simulation; the point is rather that in such games, even if the computer cheats, it cheats consistently – the problem is only a matter of cracking the rules which govern its activities. So, for the hackers, the struggle with the computer is ‹straightforward›: the attack is clean, the rules are laid down, although it is necessary to discover them, nothing inconsistent can interfere with them as in ‹real life›.

Therein consists the link of the computer world with the universe of science fiction: we conceive of a world in which all is possible, we can arrange the rules arbitrarily, the only predetermined thing is that these rules must then apply, i.e., that world must be consistent in itself. Or, as Sherry Turkle puts it: all is possible, yet nothing is contingent – what is thereby excluded, is precisely the real – impossible qua contingent encounter, tyche ... This reality, the reality of the other which is here excluded, is of course woman: the inconsistent other par excellence. The computer as partner is the means by which we evade the impossibility of the sexual relationship: a relationship with the computer is possible. Das Unheimliche (the eeriness) of the computer is exactly in that it is a machine, a consistent other, stepping into the structural position of an intersubjective partner – the computer is an ‹inhuman partner› (as Lacan says of the lady in courtly love).[7] One can also explain from this the feeling of something ‹unnatural›, obscene, almost terrible when we see children talking with a computer and obsessed with the game, oblivious of everything around them: with the computer childhood loses the last appearance of innocence.

How then to resolve the discrepancy between the computer universe as a consistent ‹regulated universe› and the fact that the hacker tries to catch the System precisely at the point of its inconsistency? The solution is elementary, almost self-evident: we simply have to distinguish between two levels, two modes of inconsistency or self-reference; the hacker's finding of the point of non-consistency, the point at which the system is caught in the trap of its own self-referentiality and starts to turn in a circle, always leaves untouched some basic consistency of the ‹regulated universe› – the self-reference at which the hacker arrives is, if we can put it thus, a consistent self-reference. The difference between the two levels of self-reference with which we are concerned is contained in Hegel's distinction between ‹bad› and ‹proper› infinity – the computer's self-referentiality remains on the level of ‹bad infinity›. We can clarify this distinction with two different paradoxes of self-reference which were both developed along the same subject, a map of England:

– first: they had an accurate map of England, on which were marked all the objects in England, thus also the map itself in relation to gradually diminishing scale, on which they again had to mark the map etc. in bad infinity; since this type of self-reference (which is today mainly familiar in the form of television pictures which are reflected by television) is an example of Hegel's bad infinity; the giddiness triggered by this vicious circle is far removed from ‹proper› infinity which is only approached by – the other version of the paradox, which we encounter – where else but in Lewis Carroll: the English decided to make an exact map of their country, but they were never completely successful in this, the map was ever more enlarged and complicated, till someone proposed that England itself could be used as its own map – and it still serves this purpose well today ... This is Hegel's ‹proper infinity›: the land itself is its own map, its own other – the flight into bad infinity does not come to an end when we reach the unattainable final link in the chain but when we recognize instead that the first link is its own other. From there we could also derive the position of the subject (in the sense of the subject of the signifier): if the land is its own map, if the original is its own model, if the thing is its own sign, then there is no positive, actual difference between them though there must be some blank space which distinguishes the thing from itself as its own sign, some non-entity which produces from the thing its sign – that ‹non-entity›, that ‹pure› difference, is the subject ... Here we have the difference between the order of sign and the order of signifier: from the sign we may obtain the signifier by including in the chain of signs ‹at least one› sign which is not simply removed from the designated thing, but marks the point at which the designated thing becomes its own sign. – The computer's self-referentiality remains on the level of ‹bad infinfity› in that it cannot reach any position of turn-around where it begins to change into its own other. And perhaps we could find in this – beyond any kind of obscurantism – the argument for the claim that ‹the computer doesn't think›.

The reason why the computer ‹doesn't think› thus keeps to the above-mentioned logic of the reverse metaphor where, instead of the computer as model for the human brain, we conceive of the brain itself as a ‹computer made of flesh and blood›; where, instead of defining the robot as the artificial man, we conceive of man proper as a ‹natural robot›, a reversal that could be further exemplified in a crucial case-in-point from the domain of sexuality. One usually considers masturbation as an ‹imaginary sexual act›, i.e. an act where bodily contact with a partner is only imagined; would it not be possible to reverse the terms and to think of the sexual act ‹proper›, the act with an ‹actual› partner, as a kind of ‹masturbation with a real (instead of only imagined) partner›? The whole point of Lacan's insistence on the «impossibility of a sexual relationship» is that this, precisely, is what the ‹actual› sexual act is (let us just recall his definition of phallic enjoyment as essentially masturbatory)! And, as we have already seen, this reference to sexuality is far from being a simple analogy: the Real whose exclusion is constitutive of what we call ‹reality›, virtual or not, is ultimately that of woman.

Our point is thus a very elementary one: true, the computer-generated ‹virtual reality› is a semblance, it does foreclose the Real in precisely the same way that, in the dream of Irma's injection, the Real is excluded by the dreamer's entry into the symbolic bliss – yet what we experience as the ‹true, hard, external reality› is based upon exactly the same exclusion. The ultimate lesson of the ‹virtual reality› is the virtualization of the very ‹true› reality: by the mirage of ‹virtual reality›, the ‹true› reality itself is posited as a semblance of itself, as a pure symbolic construct. The fact that ‹the computer doesn't think› means that the price for our access to ‹reality› is also that something must remain unthought.

NOTES

[1] Cf. Sigmund Freud, ‹Interpretation of Dreams›, Harmondsworth: Penguin Books 1977, Chapter II.

[2] ‹The Seminar of Jacques Lacan›, Book II: The Ego in Freud's Theory and in the Technique of Psychoanalyis, Cambridge: Cambridge Unversity Press 1988, p. 154-155.

[3] Ibid., p. 168.

[4] Ibid., Chapter XXIII.

[5] Cf. Sherry Turkle, ‹The Second Self. Computers and the Human Spirit›, New York: Simon and Schuster 1984; German translation ‹Die Wunschmaschine. Vom Entstehen der Computerkultur›, Reinbek bei Hamburg: Rowohlt 1984

[6] Cf. Douglas R. Hofstadter's cult-book ‹Gödel, Escher, Bach: An Eternal Golden Braid›, New York: Basic Books 1978.

[7] Turkle offers here a rather naive psychological interpretation: the subculture of the hacker is a culture of male adolescents who are running away from sexual tensions into a world of formalized ‹adventure›, in order to avoid ‹burning their fingers› with a real woman. Their attitude is inconsistent: they fear loneliness, at the same time being afraid of the approach of the other-woman, who because of her non-consistency is undependable, she can cheat, betray trust. The computer is a salvation from this dilemma: it is a partner, we are no longer alone, yet at the same time it is not threatening, it is dependable and consistent ...

Slavoj Žižek
Von der virtuellen Realität zur Virtualisierung der Realität

Wie nähert man sich der ‹virtuellen Realität› aus der Perspektive der Psychonalyse? Nehmen wir als Ausgangspunkt Freuds berühmtesten Traum, den von Irmas Injektion;[1] der erste Teil des Traums, Freuds Dialog mit Irma, dieser exemplarische Fall einer doppelten, spiegelbildlichen Beziehung, gipfelt in einem Blick in ihren offenen Mund:

«Es gibt da eine schreckliche Entdeckung, die des Fleisches, das man niemals sieht, den Grund der Dinge, die Kehrseite des Gesichts, des Antlitzes, die Sekreta par excellence, das Fleisch, aus dem alles hervorgeht, aus der tiefsten Tiefe selbst des Geheimnisses, das Fleisch, insofern es leidend ist, insofern es unförmig ist, insofern seine Form durch sich selbst etwas ist, das Angst hervorruft. Vision der Angst, Identifikation der Angst, letzte Offenbarung des *Du bist dies – Du bist dies, was am weitesten entfernt ist von dir, dies welches das Unförmigste ist.*»[2]

Dieser Schrecken geht plötzlich wundersam in ‹eine Art Ataraxie› über, die Lacan als ‹das Infunktiontreten des symbolischen Systems›[3] – exemplifiziert durch die Trimetylamin-Formel – definiert, und das Subjekt floatet frei in symbolischer Glückseligkeit. Die Falle, die es hier zu vermeiden gilt, ist natürlich, diese symbolische Glückseligkeit als Gegensatz zur ‹harten Realität› zu sehen; denn die fundamentale These der Lacanschen Psychoanalyse lautet ja im Gegenteil, daß das, was wir ‹Realität› nennen, sich vor dem Hintergrund einer solchen ‹Glückseligkeit›, d.h. einer solchen Ausgrenzung eines traumatischen Realen (hier dargestellt als der Rachen einer *Frau*), konstituiert. Genau das meint Lacan, wenn er sagt, die Phantasie sei die letztliche Stütze der Realität: Die ‹Realität› stabilisiert sich, indem irgendein Phantasiegebilde einer ‹symbolischen Glückseligkeit› den Blick in den Abgrund des Realen verhindert. Keineswegs eine Art Traumgespinst, das uns davon abhält, ‹die Realität so zu sehen, wie sie wirklich ist›, konstituiert die Phantasie vielmehr das, was wir Realität nennen. Bereits die allerselbstverständlichste körperliche ‹Realität› konstituiert sich über den Umweg durch ein Phantasiegespinst. Mit anderen Worten: der Preis, den wir für unseren Zugang zur ‹Realität› bezahlen, besteht darin, daß etwas – das Reale des Traumas – ‹verdrängt› werden muß.

Was hier ins Auge fällt, ist die Parallele zwischen dem Traum von Irmas Injektion und einem anderen berühmten Freudschen Traum – den vom toten Sohn, der seinem Vater erscheint und ihm vorwurfsvoll zuraunt: «Vater, siehst du denn nicht, daß ich verbrenne?» In seiner Interpretation des Traums von Irmas Injektion verweist Lacan auf die treffende Bemerkung von Eric Erikson, daß Freud nach dem Blick in Irmas Rachen, nach dieser Begegnung mit dem Realen, hätte erwachen müssen – so wie der Träumer des Traums vom brennenden Kind nach dem Auftreten dieser schrecklichen Erscheinung erwacht: konfrontiert mit dem Realen in seiner ganzen unerträglichen Schrecklichkeit, erwacht der Träumer, d.h. er flüchtet sich in die ‹Realität›. Aus dieser Parallele zwischen den beiden Träumen ist ein radikaler Schluß zu ziehen: Was wir ‹Realität› nennen, konstituiert sich genau nach dem Modell der eselsblöden ‹symbolischen Glückseligkeit›, die es Freud erlaubt, nach dem schrecklichen Blick in Irmas Rachen weiterzuschlafen. Der anonyme Träumer, der, um das traumatische Reale des Vorwurfs des brennenden Sohnes zu vermeiden, in die Realität erwacht, verfährt genauso wie Freud, der nach dem Blick in Irmas Rachen ‹das Register wechselt›, d.h. sich in die das Reale verschleiernde Phantasie flüchtet. – Was hat das alles mit dem Computer zu tun? Bereits 1954 wies Lacan darauf hin, daß in der heutigen Welt, in der Welt der Maschine schlechthin, der Computer den paradigmatischen Fall dieser ‹symbolischen Glückseligkeit› darstellt.[4] Man kann das feststellen, indem man eine Art phänomenologische epoché vornimmt: wenn man die (technologischen) Fragen, wie der Computer funktioniert, ausklammert und sich auf seine symbolischen Auswirkungen beschränkt, darauf, wie der Computer sich in unser symbolisches Universum einschreibt.

Mit anderen Worten: man muß den Computer als eine *machine à penser* begreifen, in dem Sinne wie Levi-Strauss von Nahrung als einem *objet à penser* und nicht einem bloßen *objet à manger* spricht. Denn aufgrund seiner ‹Unerklärlichkeit›, seiner beinahe unheimlichen Natur, ist der Computer ein ‹evokatorisches Objekt›,[5] ein Objekt, das, über seine instrumentelle Funktion hinaus, eine ganze Reihe grundlegender Fragen aufwirft, über die Besonderheit menschlichen Denkens, über den Unterschied zwischen Belebtem und Unbelebtem usw. Kein Wunder, daß die Computer-Metapher in allen möglichen Gebieten reproduziert wird und universelle Verbreitung erlangt (wir ‹programmieren› unsere Aktivitäten, aus einer Sackgasse gelangen wir mittels ‹Debugging› usw.). Der Computer ist ein drittes, neues Stadium in Marx' Entwicklungsschema, das vom Werkzeug (als Erweiterung des menschlichen Körpers) zur Maschine (die automatisch arbeitet und dem Menschen den Rhythmus vorgibt) fortschreitet: einerseits ist der Computer näher am Werkzeug, insofern er nicht von allein arbeitet, der Mensch den Rhythmus vorgibt usw.; andererseits aber ist er sogar noch selbständiger aktiv als die Maschine, da er als Partner in einem Dialog wirkt, in dem er selber Fragen aufwirft usw. Im Gegensatz zu einer mechanischen Maschine, ist das, was in seinem Inneren vorgeht, ‹intransparent›, nicht *stricto sensu* darstellbar (seine Funktionsweise läßt sich nicht wie eine Kupplung oder Gangschaltung ‹illustrieren›), und er arbeitet auf der Basis eines Dialogs mit seinem Benutzer; aus diesem Grund bewirkt er im Subjekt/Benutzer eine Spaltung des Typs ‹ich weiß, aber trotzdem ...›: Natürlich wissen wir, daß er ‹unbelebt› ist, daß er nur eine Maschine ist, aber trotzdem verhalten wir uns ihm gegenüber als ob er lebendig wäre und denken könnte ...

Wie also ‹denkt› man, jenseits seiner instrumentellen Verwendung, ‹mit dem Computer›? Ein Computer ist in seiner soziosymbolischen Wirkung nichts Eindeutiges, sondern fungiert als eine Art ‹Projektionstest›, eine Projektionsfläche der Phantasie, auf der sich das Feld unterschiedlicher sozialer Reaktionen abbildet. Zwei der wichtigsten Reaktionen sind die ‹Orwellsche› (der Computer als Inkarnation des Big Brother, als Beispiel zentralisierter totalitärer Kontrolle) und die ‹anarchistische›, welche den Computer im Gegenteil als Möglichkeit einer neuen, selbstverwalteten Gesellschaft sieht: ‹eine Kooperative des Wissens›, die jedem die Kontrolle ‹von unten› ermöglicht und damit das soziale Leben transparent und kontrollierbar macht. Gemeinsam ist diesen gegensätzlichen Reaktionen die Auffassung des Computers als Kontroll- und Beherrschungsinstrument, nur daß es sich im einen Fall um Kontrolle ‹von oben› und im anderen um Kontrolle ‹von unten› handelt. Auf der individuellen Ebene steht dieser Erfahrung des Computers als Beherrschungs- und Kontrollinstrument (als transparentes, organisiertes und kontrolliertes Universum im Gegensatz zum ‹irrationalen› sozialen Leben) seine wundersame und magische Wirkung gegenüber: Wenn es uns gelingt, mittels eines einfachen Programms einen komplexen Effekt zu erzielen, erzeugt das im Beobachter – der letzlich natürlich mit dem Benutzer selbst identisch ist – den Eindruck, daß der erzielte Effekt in keinem Verhältnis zu den bescheidenen Mitteln steht, den Eindruck eines Hiatus zwischen Ursache und Wirkung. Es ist von besonderem Interesse, wie dieser Gegensatz auf der Ebene des

Programmierens die Differenz männlich/weiblich wiederholt – in Form der Unterscheidung zwischen ‹hartem› (zwanghaftem) und ‹weichem› (hysterischem) Programmieren: ersteres zielt auf komplette Kontrolle und Beherrschung, Transparenz und analytische Zerlegung des Ganzen in seine Teile; letzteres geht intuitiv vor, improvisiert, probiert herum und entdeckt so das Neue, es läßt das Resultat selbst ‹überraschen›, seine Beziehung zum Objekt ist eher die eines ‹Dialogs› ...

Am stärksten als ‹evokatorisches Objekt› wirkt der Computer natürlich in der Frage der ‹künstlichen Intelligenz› – hier hat bereits eine Umkehrung stattgefunden, die das Schicksal jeder erfolgreichen Metapher ist: Zuerst versucht man das menschliche Denken so gut als möglich mit dem Computer zu simulieren, das Modell so nah als möglich an das menschliche ‹Original› heranzubringen, bis sich ab einem bestimmten Punkt die Dinge umkehren und die Frage erhebt: *Was, wenn das ‹Modell› bereits ein Modell des ‹Originals› selbst ist,* was, wenn die menschliche Intelligenz selbst wie ein Computer arbeitet, ‹programmiert› ist usw.? Der Computer erhebt in reiner Form die Frage des Anscheins, eines Diskurses, der kein Simulacrum wäre: es ist klar, daß der Computer in gewisser Weise Denken nur ‹simuliert›; wie *aber unterscheidet sich die totale Simulation des Denkens von ‹wirklichem› Denken?* Es ist also nicht verwunderlich, daß das Gespenst der ‹künstlichen Intelligenz› die Paradoxa des Inzestverbots auf den Plan ruft – die ‹künstliche Intelligenz› erscheint als etwas, das gleichzeitig *verboten* und als *unmöglich* angesehen wird: man behauptet, einer Maschine sei es nicht möglich zu denken, während man gleichzeitig damit beschäftigt ist, die Forschung in diese Richtung zu verbieten, mit der Begründung, es sei gefährlich, ethisch zweifelhaft usw.

Der übliche Einwand gegen die ‹künstliche Intelligenz› ist, daß der Computer letztlich nur ‹programmiert› ist, daß er nur mechanisch reproduziert, was man ihm eingibt, daß er nicht im eigentlichen Sinn des Wortes ‹verstehen› kann, wohingegen die Tätigkeit des Menschen spontan und kreativ sei. Darauf lautet die erste Antwort der Vertreter der ‹künstlichen Intelligenz›: Ist die ‹Kreativität›, ‹Spontaneität›, ‹Unvorhersagbarkeit› usw. des Menschen nicht bloß eine Erscheinung, die durch das simultane Ablaufen mehrerer Programme zustandekommt? Infolgedessen führt auch der Weg zur ‹künstlichen Intelligenz› über die Konstruktion eines Systems mit multiplen Prozessoren ... Das Hauptargument der Vertreter der ‹künstlichen Intelligenz› ist aber vor allem, daß der Computer keineswegs einer linearen, mechanischen Logik gehorcht: seine Logik ist ‹Gödelisch›, eine Logik der Selbst-Referenz, rekursiver Funktionen und Paradoxa, wo das Ganze Teil seiner selbst, auf sich selbst anwendbar ist usw. Die Idee des Computers als eine geschlossene, konsistente, lineare Maschine ist eine mechanische, ‹vorcomputerartige› Vorstellung; der Computer ist vielmehr eine inkonsistente, in den Schlingen der Selbstreferenz gefangene Maschine, die niemals totalisiert werden kann. Genau darin suchen die Proponenten der ‹Computer-Kultur› die Verbindung zwischen Wissenschaft und Kunst: in der prinzipiellen, nicht bloß empirischen Nichttotalität und Inkonsistenz des Computers. – Ist diese selbstreflexive Aktivität des Computers nicht einer Bachschen Fuge homolog, die unaufhörlich dasselbe Thema aufgreift?[6]

Diese Ideen bilden die Grundlage der Hacker-Subkultur. Hakker operieren als ein Kreis von Eingeweihten, die sich aus der ‹Normalität› des Alltags ausgrenzen, um sich dem Programmieren als Selbstzweck zu widmen; ihr Feind ist die ‹normale›, bürokratische, instrumentelle, konsistente, totalisierende Verwendung des Computers, die dessen ‹ästhetische› Dimension außer acht läßt; ihr ‹Meister-Signifikant›, ihr Manna, das Ziel, der Trick eines ‹Hack› besteht darin, ‹das System zu überlisten› (z.B. in einen geschützten, geschlossenen Informationskreislauf einzudringen). Der Hacker attackiert also das System *in dem Punkt seiner Inkonsistenz* – einen ‹Hack› anzubringen heißt, den Fehler, das Symptom des Systems ausnutzen zu können. Die universalisierte metaphorische Anwendung des

‹Hack› entspricht genau dieser Dimension: So wird z.B. in der Subkultur der Hacker das Gödelsche Theorem als ‹Gödelscher Hack› aufgefaßt, der das totalitäre logische Russel-Whitehead-System unterminierte ...

Im Gegensatz zu dieser Suche nach dem Punkt der Inkonsistenz des Systems, ist die Ästhetik des Hackers jedoch die Ästhetik eines ‹regelgeleiteten Universums›. Es ist ein Universum, das Intersubjektivität, eine Beziehung zum anderen qua Subjekt, ausschließt: Ungeachtet all der Gefahren, Anspannung und Verwunderung, die wir erleben, wenn wir in ein Videospiel vertieft sind, gibt es doch eine grundlegende Differenz zwischen dieser Art der Spannung und derjenigen in unserer Beziehung zur ‹wirklichen Welt› – eine Differenz, die nicht darin besteht, daß das computer-generierte Video ‹bloß ein Spiel› ist, eine Simulation; das Entscheidende ist vielmehr, daß der Computer bei solchen Spielen, selbst wenn er betrügt, *konsistent betrügt* – das Problem ist lediglich eine Frage des Eindringens in die Regeln, die seine Aktivitäten steuern. Für den Hacker ist also der Kampf mit dem Computer eine ‹klare› Angelegenheit: die Attacke ist sauber, die Regeln sind, auch wenn man sie erst entdecken muß, festgelegt, nichts Inkonsistentes kann dazwischen kommen wie im ‹richtigen Leben›.

Das verbindet die Computerwelt mit dem Universum der Science Fiction: wir denken uns eine Welt aus, in der alles möglich ist, wir können die Regeln willkürlich festlegen, das Einzige, was vorgegeben ist, ist, daß diese Regeln dann auch gelten müssen, d.h. daß diese Welt mit sich selbst konsistent sein muß. Oder wie Sherry Tuckle sagt: *alles ist möglich, aber nichts kontingent.* Was dabei ausgeschlossen wird, ist genau die *real-unmögliche* qua kontingente Begegnung, *tyche* ... Dieses Reale, das Reale des Anderen, das hier ausgeschlossen wird, ist natürlich die *Frau*: das inkonsistente Andere par excellence. Der Computer als Partner ist das Mittel, die Unmöglichkeit der sexuellen Beziehung zu umgehen: eine Beziehung mit dem Computer ist möglich. *Das Unheimliche* besteht genau darin, daß er eine *Maschine* ist, ein konsistentes Anderes, *das an die strukturelle Stelle des intersubjektiven Partners tritt* – der Computer ist ein ‹unmenschlicher Partner› (wie Lacan über die Dame in der höfischen Liebe sagt).[7] Von daher können wir auch unser Gefühl von etwas ‹Unnatürlichem›, Obszönem, beinahe Schrecklichem erklären, wenn wir Kinder mit dem Computer sprechen oder besessen in ein Spiel vertieft sehen, alles um sie herum vergessend: Mit dem Computer verliert die Kindheit den letzten Anschein der Unschuld.

Wie läßt sich also die Diskrepanz zwischen dem Computeruniversum als konsistentes ‹regelgeleitetes Universum› und der Tatsache, daß der Hacker das System genau am Punkt seiner Inkonsistenz zu treffen trachtet, auflösen? Die Lösung ist eine elementare, fast selbstverständliche: Wir brauchen nur zwei Ebenen, zwei Modi der Inkonsistenz oder Selbstreferenz unterscheiden; der Hacker, der den Punkt der Inkonsistenz findet, den Punkt, wo sich das System in der Falle der Selbstreferenz verfängt und im Kreis zu drehen beginnt, läßt irgendeine grundlegende Konsistenz des ‹regelgeleiteten Universums› stets unangetastet – die Selbstreferenz, auf die der Hacker stößt, ist, wenn wir so sagen können, eine konsistente Selbstreferenz. Der Unterschied zwischen den beiden Ebenen der Selbstreferenz, um die es hier geht, ist in der Hegelschen Unterscheidung zwischen ‹schlechtem› und ‹wahrem› Unendlichem enthalten – die Selbstreferenz des Computers bleibt auf der Ebene des ‹schlechten Unendlichen›. Wir können diese Unterscheidung an zwei verschiedenen Paradoxa deutlich machen, die beide am selben Gegenstand entwickelt wurden – einer Landkarte von England.

– Erstens: es gab eine genaue Karte von England, auf der man alle Objekte in England eingezeichnet hatte, also auch, in einem allmählich sich verkleinernden Verhältnis, die Landkarte selbst, auf der man wiederum die Landkarte einzeichnen mußte usw. in schlechter Unendlichkeit – denn diese Art der Selbstreferenz (die uns heute hauptsächlich in Form von in Fernsehbildern gespiegelten Fernsehbildern vertraut sind) ist ein Beispiel für das schlechte Unendliche Hegels; der Schwindel, den dieser Teufelskreis erzeugt, ist weit entfernt vom ‹wahren› Unendlichen, dem wir uns erst in

– der zweiten Version des Paradoxons nähern, der wir – wo sonst? – bei Lewis Carroll begegnen: Die Engländer beschlossen, eine genaue Karte ihres Landes anzufertigen, aber sie wollte ihnen nie vollkommen gelingen; die Karte wurde immer weiter vergrößert und kompliziert, bis jemand den Vorschlag machte, man könne doch England selbst als seine eigene Karte verwenden – und diesen Zweck erfüllt es auch heute noch gut ... Das ist Hegels ‹wahres Unendliches›: das Land selbst ist seine eigene Landkarte, sein eigenes Anderes – die Flucht ins schlechte Unendliche endet nicht, wenn wir das unerreichbare letzte Glied der Kette erreichen, sondern wenn wir erkennen, daß schon das erste Glied sein eigenes Anderes ist. Von da aus können wir auch den Ort des Subjekts (im Sinn von ‹das Subjekt des Signifikanten›) herleiten: Wenn das Land seine eigene Landkarte ist, das Original sein eigenes Modell, das Ding sein eigenes Zeichen, dann gibt es zwischen ihnen keine positive, wirkliche Differenz; wohl aber muß es irgendeine leere Distanz geben, die das Ding von sich selbst als seinem Zeichen unterscheidet – irgendein ‹Nicht-Ding›, das aus dem *Ding dessen Zeichen macht.* Dieses ‹Nicht-Ding›, diese ‹reine› Differenz ist das Subjekt ... Hier haben wir die Differenz zwischen der Ordnung des Zeichens und der Ordnung des *Signifikanten:* vom Zeichen zum Signifikanten gelangen wir, indem wir in die Kette der Zeichen ‹zumindest *ein*› Zeichen aufnehmen, das sich nicht einfach in Distanz zum bezeichneten Ding befindet, sondern den Punkt markiert, an dem das bezeichnete Ding zu seinem eigenen Zeichen wird. Die Selbstreferenz des Computers bleibt insofern auf der Ebene des ‹schlechten Unendlichen›, als sie nicht bis zu der Stelle reicht, wo der Ausgangspunkt sie in ihr eigenes Anderes verwandelt. Und vielleicht ließe sich darin auch – jenseits allen Obskurantismus – das Argument für die Behauptung sehen, daß ‹der Computer nicht denkt›.

Die Begründung, warum der Computer ‹nicht denkt›, hält sich damit an die oben erwähnte Logik der Metaphernumkehrung, wonach wir, statt den Computer als Modell des menschlichen Gehirns zu sehen, das Gehirn selbst als einen ‹Computer aus Fleisch und Blut› begreifen, statt den Roboter als künstlichen Menschen zu definieren, den Menschen selbst als einen ‹natürlichen Roboter› auffassen – eine Umkehrung die sich weiter exemplifizieren ließe an einem zentralen Beispiel aus dem Bereich der Sexualität: Üblicherweise betrachtet man die Masturbation als einen ‹imaginären Geschlechtsakt›, d.h. einen Geschlechtsakt, bei dem der Körperkontakt mit einem Partner bloß imaginiert wird; wäre es nicht möglich die Begriffe umzukehren und den ‹eigentlichen› Geschlechtsakt, den Akt mit einem ‹tatsächlichen› Partner, als eine Art ‹Masturbation mit einem realen (statt bloß imaginierten) Partner› zu sehen? Das Entscheidende an Lacans Insistieren auf der ‹Unmöglichkeit der sexuellen Beziehung› ist ja, daß der ‹tatsächliche› Geschlechtsakt genau das ist (denken wir nur an seine Definition des phallischen Genusses als essentiell masturbatorisch)! Und dieser Hinweis auf die Sexualität ist, wie wir bereits gesehen haben, keineswegs nur eine bloße Analogie: das Reale, dessen Ausgrenzung für das, was wir ‹Realität› nennen, ob nun virtuell oder nicht, konstitutiv ist, ist letzlich das Reale der *Frau*.

Worauf wir hier hinaus wollen, ist also etwas sehr Elementares: Ohne Frage, die computer-generierte ‹virtuelle Realität› ist eine Simulation, sie schließt das Reale genauso aus wie es im Traum von Irmas Injektion durch den Eintritt des Träumers in die symbolische Glückseligkeit ausgeschlossen wird – aber was wir als die ‹wirkliche, harte, äußere Realität› erleben beruht auf genau derselben Ausgrenzung. Die Lektion der ‹virtuellen Realität› ist letztlich die Virtualisierung der ‹wirklichen› Realität: Durch das Trugbild der ‹virtuellen Realität› wird auch die ‹wirkliche› Realität als ein Simulacrum ihrer selbst hingestellt, als ein rein symbolisches Konstrukt. Die Tatsache, daß ‹der Computer nicht denkt›, heißt, daß der Preis für unseren Zugang zur ‹Realität› ebenfalls darin besteht, daß *etwas ungedacht bleiben muß.*

ANMERKUNGEN

[1] Vgl. Sigmund Freud, *Die Traumdeutung*, Studienausgabe, Bd. 2, Frankfurt/M.: S. Fischer 1969 – 1975, II. Kapitel.

[2] *Das Seminar von Jaques Lacan, Buch II: Das Ich in der Theorie Freuds und in der Technik der Psychoanalyse,* Übers. v. Hans-Joachim Metzger, Olten u. Freiburg i. Br.: Walter 1980, S. 199f.

[3] Ibid., S. 215f.

[4] Ibid., Kapitel XXIII.

[5] Vgl. Sherry Tuckle, *Die Wunschmaschine. Der Computer als zweites Ich,* Reinbeck: Rowohlt 1986 (=rororo 8135).

[6] Vgl. Douglas R. Hofstadters Kultbuch *Gödel, Escher, Bach. Ein Endloses Geflochtenes Band,* Stuttgart: Klett-Cotta 1985.

[7] Turkle bietet hier eine eher naive psychologische Interpretation: Die Subkultur der Hacker ist eine Welt männlicher Jugendlicher, die sich vor sexuellen Spannungen in eine Welt formalisierter ‹Abenteuer› flüchtet, um sich nicht mit einer wirklichen Frau ‹die Finger zu verbrennen›. Ihre Haltung ist eine inkonsistente: Sie fürchten sich vor Einsamkeit und haben gleichzeitig Angst, sich dem Anderen/der Frau zu nähern, die aufgrund ihrer Inkonsistenz unverläßlich ist, betrügen, das Vertrauen enttäuschen kann. Der Computer ist ein Ausweg aus diesem Dilemma: er ist ein Partner, wir sind nicht mehr allein, und er ist gleichzeitig unbedrohlich, verläßlich und konsistent ...

Friedrich A. Kittler
Gespräch zwischen Peter Weibel und Friedrich A. Kittler

Weibel: Wie würdest Du den Unterschied zwischen Schreibmaschine und Computer bezeichnen?
Kittler: Bevor man auf die Unterschiede zu sprechen kommt, ist erst einmal dieser triviale, aber nicht ganz unnötige Satz zu sagen, daß es mehr Gemeinsamkeiten zwischen den beiden Geräten gibt, als gemeinhin bekannt ist. Wenn es stimmt, was Andrew Hodges erzählt, daß der arme kleine Junge Alan Turing, Erfinder aller Computer, eine so schlechte Handschrift und mit ihr auf englischen Public Schools keinerlei Erfolgschance hatte, resultiert das Konzept der ersten Universalen Diskreten Maschine unmittelbar aus den gescheiterten Schreibmaschinenentwürfen, die Turing mit 14 Jahren machte. Diese Anekdote läßt schon erkennen, wie nahe beieinander die Dinge liegen: Die totale Durchstandardisierung der Schrift und ihrer Zeichen beginnt wirklich mit der Schreibmaschine, die die Handschrift ab 1870 nicht nur im Druckgewerbe, was ja eine sehr öffentliche Angelegenheit geblieben war, sondern an jedem einzelnen Arbeitsplatz und Schreibtisch abgelöst hat, während der Computer diese Standardisierung der Zeichen auf radikale Weise fortsetzt. Er standardisiert nicht nur die Zeichen, sondern analysiert auch ihre Menge, bis sich frei nach dem Motto der Telegraphie herausstellt, daß zwei Zeichen schlechthin hinreichen. Die 26 Buchstaben plus Spatium als Minimalausstattung einer Schreibmaschinentastatur, die ja in Reming-

tons Anfängen noch ohne Großbuchstaben auskommen mußte, schrumpfen dann auf das Zeichenpaar '0' und '1'. Diese Binarisierung aber eröffnet ganz neue Speicher- und Verarbeitungsmöglichkeiten. Denn solange man bei einer zufällig aufgerafften Menge von soundsoviel griechischen oder lateinischen Buchstaben stehenbleibt, sind Operationen immer nur möglich als Gliederung eines chaotischen Bereiches jenseits von Schrift – etwa der Stimme. Die Buchstaben selber können im Ernst nicht mehr miteinander interagieren, sondern sie sind so, weil sie historisch so geworden sind. Demgegenüber lassen sich die zwei Schreibzustände, die das physikalische Korrelat der binären Zeichen '0' und '1' abgeben, wieder miteinander rückkoppeln, was man sich bei Buchstaben überhaupt nicht vorstellen könnte. Was hieße es, 'a' und 'b' miteinander rückzukoppeln? Man kann aber sehr wohl '0' und '1' als Sequenz miteinander rückkoppeln. Daraus folgen all jene Unterschiede, die dafür gesorgt haben, daß die Schreibmaschine und alle anderen Schriftsysteme eben lediglich Speichermedien sind und bleiben, wohingegen der Computer über Speicherungsfunktionen hinaus auch die Funktionen der Übertragung und der Berechnung von Daten, also ihre Berechnung und Manipulation übernimmt. Leichtsinnig könnte man sagen, er ist eine Schreibmaschine, die nicht bloß schreibt, sondern sich auch selbst liest.

Weibel: Kann man sagen, daß diese Standardisierung auf zwei Werte aber auch gleichzeitig eine Universalisierung bedeutet hat? Mit der Schreibmaschine konnte ich ja nur Text erzeugen, mit dem Computer auch Bilder. Sind Bild und Text aber nur Codes, die einem universalen binären Code unterworfen sind und kann ich dadurch mit dem Computer nicht nur Texte, sondern auch Bild erzeugen?

Kittler: Das ist eine schwierige Frage, wenn man neben der heute so faszinierenden Bildgenerierung auch die Sounderzeugung nicht übersieht, die ja mittlerweile ebenso perfektioniert wie vergessen scheint. Zum Beispiel hat schon der uralte Telegraph, der im 19. Jahrhundert auf perforierten Bändern mit Löchern, Strichen usw. lief, Musik gemacht, wenn man die Bänder nur schneller ablaufen ließ, als Menschen schreiben oder lesen konnten. Genau diese Tatsache, daß Telegraphenapparate dann in unterschiedlichen Frequenzen und Tonhöhen summen oder brummen, brachte Edison bekanntlich 1877 zur Erfindung eines ersten Grammophonvorläufers, des Phonographen. Insofern ist durch Mißbrauch von Geräten prinzipiell immer eine Möglichkeit gegeben, mit Dingen anders als bloß textuell umzugehen. Und das Paradoxe bei der computerisierten Erzeugung von Bildern oder Sounds ist wohl, daß erst andere Medientechnologien kategoriale Umstürze oder Revolutionen im Begriff vom Bild oder Geräusch bewerkstelligen mußten, bis es möglich wurde, daß der Computer als solcher zur Bildproduktion antrat. Revolution soll dabei heißen, daß man auch die Bilder nach dem Modell der Buchstaben erstmals in der Geschichte als Mengen von endlich vielen Elementen aufgefaßt hat, also als Cantorscher Staub und dergleichen. Bezeichnenderweise war Georg Cantor mit seinen mathematischen Punktmengen ein Zeitgenosse der Pointillisten, die Bilder gleichfalls in Punkte auflösten, und des Physikstudenten Paul Nipkow, der am Weihnachtstag 1884 in seiner Berliner Bude das Prinzip des Fernsehens als einer diskreten Abtastung von Bildern entwickelt hat. Das war der Film ja noch nicht gewesen, weil er zwar zwischen den einzelnen Aufnahmen Schnitte machte, aber die einzelnen Aufnahmen doch noch als Kontinua, als reelle Zahlen aufnahm und wiedergab. Deshalb hat eigentlich erst die Revolution, die reelle Zahlen mit ihren unendlich vielen Kommastellen durch abzählbare Mengen ganzer Zahlen ersetzte, die moderne Bildermanipulation ermöglicht. John von Neumanns großartiger Hinweis, daß die Messungen reeller Zahlen und analoger Computer immer mit Rauschfehlern behaftet sind, wohingegen der Rundungsfehler bei digitalisierten Zahlen beliebig klein gemacht, das Rauschen also gegen Null gebracht werden kann, scheint die theoretische Basis dafür, daß es heute so etwas wie Imaging gibt. Und die CDs sind der erste historische Effekt der Tatsache, daß man durch Zerhackung, also durch Verunstaltung von Signalen bessere Signale erzeugt als durch diese analoge Treue, die das Grammophon zeitlebens gewahrt hat.

Weibel: Ist für Dich dann der Computer der erste Schritt zu einer Standardisierung des Sehens wie vorhin die Schreibmaschine zur Standardisierung der Schrift?

Kittler: Ja, die Bilder sind der letzte Schritt. Man kann die Pixelwelt am Fernsehen als Vorbereitung auf den Computer auffassen oder meinetwegen auch das wohl erst im 19. Jahrhundert erfundene Prinzip des Dithering in der Druckgraphik. Lange bevor die Computer anfingen, Punkte zu mischen, weil sie für Photorealismus noch nicht genügend Farben hatten, haben ja schon die Graphiker, vor allem die Photozeitungsreproduktionstechniker des 19. Jahrhunderts diesen Begriff von Pixeln entwickelt, also einfach Graupunkte eingesetzt, die, mehr oder minder zufällig verteilt, aus der Entfernung betrachtet dann doch ein Gesicht ergeben. Aber diese Theoriepraxis des Sehens schlägt der gesamten europäischen Sehweise seit Platon ins Gesicht.

Weibel: Würdest Du sagen, daß im 19. Jahrhundert, vom Pointillismus bis zur Reproduktionstechnik, schon grundlegende Vorarbeiten zur Alphabetisierung des Bildes gemacht worden sind, d.h. daß man versucht hat, das Bild auch in Einzelpunkte zu zerlegen wie vorher die Schrift in Buchstaben, und daß schon vor 1900 das Terrain zur Mathematisierung des Bildes vorbereitet wurde?

Kittler: Ja. Die Prinzipien wurden damals aufgestellt, auch wenn einige Gleichungen oder Algorithmen der digitalen Bildverarbeitung keine zehn Jahre alt sind. Und vielleicht mußte noch etwas dazu kommen, was seit 1917 in der Theorie zirkuliert, aber erst durch Norbert Wiener wahrhaft berühmt geworden ist, nämlich die Rückkopplung als Möglichkeit, Bilder auf Bilder zurückzuführen oder die mathematische Repräsentation eines Bildes wieder auf das Bild anzuwenden. Man kann seitdem Bilder von Bildern berechnen, zum Beispiel ein Bild mit sich selbst autokorrelieren oder einer Fourier-Transformation unterziehen. Das scheinen die wirklich neuen Möglichkeiten zu sein, die das Bild im Unterschied zur Tradition nicht mehr als Gegebenheit, als Datum behandeln, sondern als Zwischenstadium in einem mathematischen Prozeß.

Weibel: Ich glaube auch, daß die Subjekt-Objekt Trennung beim Computer noch viel unschärfer ist als bei der Schreibmaschine. Eben wenn das Bild sich selbst schon beschreibt oder ein Bild vom Bild machen kann, wird da das Bild sein eigener Beobachter? Und tangiert das auch unsere eigene Beobachtung, wie wir dem Bild gegenüber stehen?

Kittler: Ja. Keine der traditionellen Maschinen hat eben alle menschlichen Funktionen ergänzen oder supplementieren oder ersetzen können, sondern alle waren Teilaspekte, wenn man das überhaupt noch anthropologisch oder anthropomorph betrachten darf, was ich nur zögernd tue. Erst der Computer ist ein selbstgesteuertes System, ein Subjekt im kantischen Sinn, mit allen möglichen ‹Vermögen› des sogenannten Menschen ausgestattet. Er bringt es bei der Bildanalyse bis zur Urteilskraft, sogar bis zur reflektierenden. Eben darum verschwinden wir als Subjekte ziemlich vollständig. Die Programme werden mehr und mehr sich selbst steuern und alle Tendenzen, die jetzt auch und gerade in der Computerpraxis dahingehen, die textbezogenen Kommandozeilen und Befehlslogiken durch bildgesteuerte Programme – vom grauenhaften Windows unter DOS bis hin zu X Window unter UNIX – zu ersetzen, erzeugen ja als Bilder einen derart dichten Vorhang vor dem, was immer noch Zeichensystem im Inneren der Schaltkreise ist, daß die Benutzer mehr oder minder zu Haustieren degradiert werden, denn durch eine graphische Benutzeroberfläche kommt man einfach nicht mehr zum System-Code durch.

Weibel: Was bedeutet das für Dich in der Theorie, daß das Bild und der Beobachter sich gleichzeitig und gegenseitig verändern? Bei der Schreibmaschine war das ja nicht der Fall. Mit der Computertechnologie wird das Bild durch den bloßen Akt des Beobachtens verändert. Es gibt diese Möglichkeit, daß dieser Beobachterzustand elektromagnetisch gespeichert wird und sofort wiederum das Bild beeinflußt.

Kittler: Willst Du sagen, der Beobachter beeinflußt das Bild?

Weibel: Ist möglich, ja.

Kittler: Das zu implementieren, indem man eine Schreibmaschine als Fußboden auslegt, ist vielleicht machbar, aber ich glaube nicht, daß das der Normalfall ist, es sei denn jetzt in den Virtual Realities, wo die Augenbewegungen selber abgetastet werden.

Weibel: Das meine ich. Was bedeutet das jetzt für Dich, für Deine Theorie?

Kittler: Ich war noch nie in einer Virtual Reality und bin auch nicht besonders gierig darauf hineinzustürzen. Was bedeutet das für meine Theorie? Meine Theorie ist gar nicht so lebensverbunden, um über alles zu reden.

Weibel: Oder sagen wir so, für die Schnittstelle, für die Theorie der Schnittstelle, was bedeutet das für Dich?

Kittler: Ich würde fast vermuten, daß bei diesen Abtastungen der berühmten Augenbewegungen oder Ophtalmokinesen, auf denen ja schon Husserl seine ganze Theorie der menschlichen Wahrnehmung aufgebaut hat, eben nicht mehr der Mensch der Beobachter ist, sondern zum ersten Mal der Beobachtete wird. Seine eigenen Beobachtungsakte, also Augenbewegungen werden ihrerseits von Sensoren beobachtet, die direkt vor dem Auge sitzen und dessen Bewegungen an die Maschine zurückmelden, woraufhin die Maschine erneut reagieren kann. Augen und Mund, die ja weithin als letzte Refugien der sogenannten Intimität gelten, werden also eingespeist in eine Rückkopplungslogik, die nicht unsere, sondern die der Maschine ist. Der Effekt von virtuellen Realitäten wäre nicht so schwindelerregend, wenn wir nicht merken würden, daß wir jetzt plötzlich gesehen werden von etwas, was wir im alteuropäischen Sinn als Subjekt oder Person nicht anerkennen können und das trotzdem ständig zeigt, daß es, ohne sich selbst zu zeigen, uns sieht.

Weibel: Das heißt, für Dich ist es eine Art weitere Verselbständigung der Autonomie der Maschine?

Kittler: Ja. Ich bin paranoisch, wie man weiß.

Weibel: Wie würdest Du das im Zusammenhang mit dem berühmten Projekt der Moderne sehen, diese Verselbständigung der Maschine, der Autonomie der Maschine?

Kittler: Dies berühmte ‹Projekt der Moderne› habe ich mir immer übersetzt als Projekt, das totale Projektil herzustellen. Deshalb fahren wir ja am 3. Oktober 1992 nach Peenemünde, um die V2 als Projektil aller Projektile zu ihrem 50. Geburtstag zu beglückwünschen. Um es mit Thomas Pynchon, dem Romancier der V2, zu sagen: das Projekt der Moderne ist im wesentlichen ein rüstungstechnisches und nachrichtentechnisches Projekt, und wenn es sich in so hübsche Formeln wie Demokratie oder kommunikativer Konsens kleidet, dann umso besser für die Leute, die das glauben.

Weibel: Wie erklärst Du Dir dann diesen ideologischen Widerstand gegen die Maschine im Projekt der Moderne? 1839 hat Fox Talbot gesehen, daß die Maschine jetzt auch das Bild selbst macht (‹it is the picture that makes itself›). Er schreibt wortwörtlich: ‹Some Account of the Art of the Photogenic Drawing, or, the Process by which Natural Objects May be Made to Delineate themselves without the Aid of the Artist's Pencil›. Aber 1844 hat er seinem Buch den Titel ‹The Pencil of Nature› gegeben statt ‹The Pencil of Machine›. Er konnte nicht zugeben, daß der Künstler ersetzt wird durch eine Maschine. Aber die Selbständigkeit der Maschine war der Beginn des Projektes der Moderne; sie hat diese ganze Logik der Autonomie, der Unabhängigkeit von Form und Farbe usw. in Gang gesetzt. Trotzdem versucht der Kulturbetrieb, die Maschine aus der Kunst herauszuhalten. Was sind das für Ängste, daß die Leute eben nicht sehen, daß das Projekt der Moderne eben ein Projektil auch mit

einer Revolution der Maschine angefangen hat. Woher kommen diese Widerstände.
Kittler: Ich würde das ziemlich institutionsgeschichtlich beantworten, nur daß über die betroffenen Institutionen noch viele Recherchen notwendig sind. Vorderhand nehme ich an, daß im 18. und 19. Jahrhundert der Konflikt zwischen den neuen Ingenieurswissenschaften einerseits, die ja weitgehend, wie etwa die École polytechnique in Paris, aus militärischen Gründen ins Leben gerufen wurden, um die faktische Arbeit der Modernisierung zu leisten, und andererseits den Universitäten, die weiterhin zumindest über ihre Lohnschreiber die Öffentlichkeit besetzt hielten, so heftig tobte, daß es für diese neuen Praxiswissenschaften ganz schwierig war, das ihrer Leistung angemessene kulturelle standing zu erlangen. In Deutschland etwa mußte erst Wilhelm II., dieser vielgeschmähte und sehr technikbegabte Kaiser, mit äußerster Gewalt dafür sorgen, daß die TH Charlottenburg ab 1900 Promotionen austeilen konnte. Sämtliche Universitäten Deutschlands sind damals auf die Barrikaden gegangen und haben dagegen protestiert, daß es überhaupt eine Öffentlichkeit der Ingenieure geben konnte. Dieser Konflikt wird wohl noch heute geschürt von Leuten, die in Frankfurt sitzen und behaupten, daß Sprache eine Seite der Kultur ist und Technik eine ganz andere. Sie begreifen also überhaupt nicht, daß alles, was wir jetzt bereden, Sprache und Schreiben, Sprache und Schreibmaschine, Sprache und Grammatik, Sprache und Codierung, ja schon Beweise genug dafür liefert, daß die Sprache selber Technik oder Technologie im weitesten Sinn ist. Es muß ein aus der Gründerzeit überkommener Begriff von Kultur und Sprache sein, der das zu sehen verhindert, besonders in Europa. Da in Japan dieser Begriff nicht herrschte, sind die Dinge viel einfacher gelaufen.
Weibel: Das finde ich auch zentral, diese These, daß die Technik selbst Sprache ist und Sprache selbst schon eine Technik ist. Könntest Du das noch ein bißchen ausführen?
Kittler: Wir können natürlich irgendwo eine Eiszeitursprache

annehmen, die lediglich ein vergehender Hauch der Stimme war, ‹ein Dasein, das verschwindet, indem es ist›, wie Hegel es genannt hätte: diese reine Stimme, die sofort abbricht, weil kein Grammophon sie auffängt. Aber eigentlich glaubt heute niemand mehr, daß es irgendwo die spontane Sprache am Anfang gegeben hätte, sondern wir sind alle überzeugt, daß zum Sprechen irgendein Zeichensystem, irgendeine Kritzelei, irgendein Graphismus, irgendeine Schrift immer schon gehört haben muß, weil Sprache ohne Gedächtnisstützen, sozusagen ohne parallele Speichertechniken sofort wieder von der Welt verschwunden wäre. Sofern und solange es Zeichensysteme gibt, die diesen seltsamen Strom der Rede, der nach Homers Wort aus dem Gehege der Lippen kommt, zerschneiden und zerhakken, um ihn memorierbar zu machen in Alphabeten oder Piktogrammen oder dergleichen, da widerfährt der Sprache, von der Schrift her gesehen, nichts anderes, als was der bunten Vielfalt der optischen Erscheinungen widerfährt, wenn der Film sie mit seinen 24 Aufnahmen pro Sekunde zerhackt. Und weil das beim Film eindeutig technisch ist, sehe ich kein Problem, diesen Begriff von Technik auf die Sprache zu übertragen. Schon die Einführung des griechischen Vokalalphabets, von dem wir ja ausgehen, insofern alle Schreibmaschinen auf diesem Alphabet, dieser virtuosen Analyse einer ‹natürlichen› Sprache beruhen, zeigt deutlich genug, daß das Sprechen selber sich durch Einführung der Schrift verändert hat. Wenn also Demokratie, Philosophie, Literatur, all diese Seltsamkeiten, die den Griechen zum ersten Mal beschert worden sind, von der Schrift ermöglicht wurden und in alphabetlosen Kulturen gar nicht aufgetreten sind, hat die Sprache an der Schrift ihr Wesen und unter anderen Zeichencodes dann auch andere Strukturen.

Weibel: Bedeutet dann der binäre Code den Endpunkt der Schrift?

Kittler: Es ist eher ein Wendepunkt. Es ist kein Ende. Und das große Problem ist ja heute, wie wir uns und unsere Zuhörer und Konsumenten dazu bringen, ernst zu machen mit diesem neuen

Zeichensystem, statt immer nur seine Effekte zu genießen. Meine Sorge bei den virtuellen Realitäten ist ja, daß die Leute sich alle in die Effekte des Computers hineinziehen lassen, während nur sehr wenige sich die wirklich mönchische Mühe machen, das Zeichensystem selbst zu erlernen. Diese mönchische Mühe namens Programmieren wird aber leider Gottes durch Macht beglichen oder bezahlt und die paar Leute, die Programme schreiben können ...

Weibel: Beginnt vielleicht sogar ein neues Zeitalter der Schrift mit diesem binären Code?

Kittler: Ja. Siehst Du jenseits des binären Codes neue Codes oder analoge Techniken aufziehen? Ich frage deshalb, weil es so schrecklich mühsam ist, obwohl mittlerweile schon viele Anstrengungen gemacht werden, um aus dieser primitivsten aller Codierungen wieder herauszukommen.

Weibel: Das heißt, die Schrift ist dann so mächtig, daß sie quasi sogar Bilder sein kann.

Kittler: Ja. Man muß vielleicht im Sinn des toten Flusser dazu sagen, daß die Schrift deshalb so mächtig ist, weil sie zum ersten Mal auch Bilder erzeugen kann, wo doch die Bilder vorher immer das Andere der Schrift waren, siehe etwa den Krieg zwischen Jesuiten und Protestanten, Camera obscura und Bibellektüre. Die Schrift von heute dagegen kann Bilder oder Töne generieren, eben weil der Unterschied zwischen Buchstaben und Zahlen im digitalen Code verschwindet.

Das war ja immer eine seltsame Geschichte. Vermutlich gab es keine europäische Schrift, die nicht auch irgendwie Zahlen mit geführt hätte, sei es, daß wie im Griechischen das Alpha als erster Buchstabe zugleich 1 bedeutete und Beta als zweiter zugleich 2, sei es wie bei den Lateinern, daß merkwürdige Striche ein Zahlensystem vertraten, oder schließlich wie seit dem Mittelalter, als man die arabischen Ziffern importierte. Aber die Trennung zwischen Buchstaben und Zahlen bestand eigentlich immer: Nationalsprachlich waren die Buchstaben, die Zahlen waren international und dafür nicht aussprechbar. Jetzt dage-

gen kann zum ersten Mal ein Signal als Buchstabe oder als Zahl gelesen werden, zwar nicht von Menschen, aber von Computern, die wir ja sich selbst lesende Schreibmaschinen nannten. Intern, auf der Hardware-Ebene, wird zwar grundsätzlich alles als Zahl oder Signalfluß gelesen, aber auch die Repräsentation von Buchstaben durch Zahlen läßt sich machen, wohingegen die umgekehrte Repräsentation von Zahlen durch Buchstaben – das, was ältere Zeiten offenbar wollten – gescheitert ist.
Weibel: Aber trotzdem kann man sagen, daß der Traum von Lullus bis Leibniz, eine Universalsprache, jetzt existiert?
Kittler: Sie existiert und Leibniz hat sie uns ja auch beschert, als binäres Zahlensystem.
Weibel: Das heißt, die Buchstaben werden als Ziffern und als Zahlensystem abgebildet. Dieses Zahlensystem ist wiederum imstande, Bilder zu erzeugen?
Kittler: Die Perspektive war ja der erste Fall, wo geometrische Systeme (noch keine algebraischen) Bilder erzeugt haben. Ich nehme an – darüber müßte man aber länger sprechen, weil es wohl auch mit Deinem Environment zu tun hat –, daß diese größere Macht der Zahlen aus ihrer unbeschränkten Manipulierbarkeit folgt. Bei Buchstaben kontrollieren wir sozusagen immer noch, was in unseren Stimmen aussprechbar ist, und beziehen es zurück auf die Semantik oder Syntax dessen, was wir reden und was uns von unseren Eltern oder Großeltern als Sprache überliefert worden ist. Bei Zahlen kann einfach irgendein Mathematiker oder Gangster hingehen und sagen, daß die Zahl 1 fortan Wurzel aus -1 bedeutet, obwohl das eigentlich für altmodische Menschen überhaupt keinen Sinn macht, diese Wurzel aus -1; oder man kann das Integralzeichen beschließen oder das Divisionszeichen ändern, wie das Leibniz gemacht hat, man kann neue Verbundsysteme aus solchen Zeichen entwikkeln, man kann Indizies weglassen, was Einstein für die Tensorrechnung gemacht hat, und man kann alle Alphabete ausbeuten. Cantor z. B. für seine Mengentheorie hat die hebräischen Zahlen in die Mathematik eingeführt. Es gibt keine Schranke für

solche Hierarchiebildungen und Zeichenstiftungen mehr. Vielleicht ist das die erste postmoderne Erscheinung, wenn man so will: Sämtliche Zeichensysteme aller Völker stehen zu willkürlichen mathematischen Neudefinitionen zur Verfügung, es ist keine Schranke gezogen, was man eigentlich alles noch als Symbol definieren könnte, d.h. als Operator.

Weibel: Ist damit die Whorf-Hypothese erledigt, daß spezifische Sprachen eine spezifische Welt schaffen? Denn die Welt des binären Code ist für alle gleich und für alle zugänglich.

Kittler: Vielleicht gibt es kleine Akzeptanzunterschiede, wie man sich heutzutage ausdrückt: Die vornehme, gepflegte Syntax des Französischen, die ja von der Académie Française zu Richelieus Zeiten und nicht erst gestern festgelegt wurde, sträubt sich am massivsten gegen die Übernahme des Computerdenkens. Im Französischen herrschen zuviele syntaktische Abhängigkeiten, um dem Computer mit seinem agglutinierenden Prinzip, wie die Sprachwissenschaft sagen würde, wo alles neben allem bestehen darf, Eingang in eine Grammatik zu gestatten, die wesentlich aus Exklusionsregeln besteht. Insofern, denke ich, gibt es heute noch nationale Differenzen in der Akzeptanz dieser Allgemeinheit.

Weibel: Aber diese Metaphysik der Sprache à la Heidegger, die Sprache als ‹Haus des Seins› funktioniert ja nicht mehr im Zeitalter der Techno-Transformation der Welt.

Kittler: Man wird mich nie dazu bringen, ein Wort gegen Heidegger zu sagen.

Weibel: Gut, dann habe ich noch eine Frage zu dem Code-Problem. Die Buchstaben, die ein Wort formen, sind ja nur dann verständlich, oder haben eine Bedeutung nur für denjenigen, der diese Sprache bewohnt und sie kennt. Anders ist es, wenn ich jetzt Französisch spreche und Du diese Sprache nicht kennst, dann haben diese Worte keine Bedeutung. Jetzt, bei diesem Code meiner Installation ist es so, daß die gleiche Geste (das Treten auf einen Sensor) in drei verschiedenen Welten verschiedene Bedeutungen hat. Ich mache immer das Gleiche, ich nehme immer das gleiche Element des Codes, nur zeige ich damit drei verschiedene Aktivitäten, drei verschiedene Formen oder World-Modes (drei verschiedene Welten). Das war bisher in der Sprache nicht der Fall.

Kittler: In der Schrift schon. Der klassische Fall wäre die Einführung der Umschalttaste bei der Schreibmaschine, um aus dem Universum der Minuskeln in das Universum der Majuskeln zu wechseln. Beim Computer ist das noch weiter getrieben. Da gibt es ja außer der Umschalttaste für Groß und Klein an jeder PC- oder AT-Tastatur noch Umschaltmöglichkeiten zwischen Texteingabe und Kommandoeingabe. Man drückt auf Control oder auf Alt, also Alternate, und der nächste eingetastete Buchstabe gilt nicht mehr als Zeichen, das einfach eine Nachricht ist, sondern als Befehl, der aktualiter tut, was das Zeichen ist. Die Eingabe fungiert dann wie ein Speech-Act, aber einer des Computers und nicht mehr des Menschen.

Allgemein würde auch ich sagen, daß es in der Sprache, wenn man sie von einer fiktiven Mündlichkeit her beschreibt, eigentlich überhaupt keine solchen Stufungen gegeben hat. Wenn man aber von vorneherein sagt, daß Sprache und Schrift einen technischen Verbund gebildet haben, müßte man eigentlich zu jeder gegebenen historischen Zeit prüfen, wie ihre Umschaltmöglichkeiten funktioniert haben. Ich denke an königliche Unterschriften oder dergleichen: Die römischen Kaiser zum Beispiel haben eine bestimmte Zeit lang als einzige Menschen mit roter Tinte schreiben dürfen und müssen, damit ihr Schreiben von vornherein eine andere Welt indizierte und eben das auslöste, was sie sagten. So ähnlich sehe ich Deine Umschaltung zwischen verschiedenen Welten als eine sehr skripturale Operation.

Weibel: Man könnte vielleicht so sagen, daß eine durch die Schreibmaschine schon vorhandene latente Möglichkeit durch den Computer enorm verstärkt wird. Nämlich, daß man nicht nur Zugang hat zu verschiedenen Welten, sondern daß man diese verschiedenen Welten kreiert. Bei der Schreibmaschine hießen diese ‹World Modes› immer nur Versalien oder Kleinschreibung oder ‹ö und e›, aber durch den Computer ist diese Möglichkeit ausgebaut worden, sodaß man faktisch die tatsächliche Kreation mehrerer Welten schaffen kann. Nachdem diese aber nicht gleichzeitig alle real sein können, müssen sie virtuelle Welten werden.

Kittler: Ja. Die Umschaltung zwischen Welten ist schon neu. Die Umschaltbarkeit als Prinzip sozusagen von Metasprache und Objektsprache habe ich mit meinen Beispielen jetzt etwas weiter zurückzuverfolgen versucht. Aber daß das ins Unendliche hinein wuchern kann, ist erst mit unseren Rechenkapazitäten möglich.

Weibel: Siehst Du da eine Gefahr für Dich, in diesem Wuchern virtueller Welten?

Kittler: Es gibt da eine Gefahr ... Ich habe auch eine recht präzise Vorstellung von dem, was virtuelle Welten sein sollten für mich. Ich komme ja vom Lötkolben her und habe meine ersten Intel-Computer-Chips selber zusammengelötet, auf ziemlich illegitime Weise in den Augen von Intel, obwohl mein Wildwuchs lief. Auch was ich mir von Virtual Realities wünschen würde, ist in den Augen der Industrie ziemlich illegitim.

Für die Gefahr halte ich, daß die Virtual Realities alle möglichen Ferienparadiese von den Malediven bis nach Madagaskar simulieren werden, aber keiner außer mir wird auf den Gedanken kommen, die Innereien des Computers selbst als virtuelle Realität für den Benutzer zu implementieren. Ich könnte mir das so schön vorstellen: Ich würde hineingehen, würde mich langsam von den Hochsprachenebenen hinuntertasten bis auf die Assemblerebene, auf die Objektcodeebene, auf die Hardwareebene, und dann könnte ich mit dem virtuellen Lötkolben hinein in meine Maschine, wenn sie sich mir selber virtuell repräsentieren würde, und schließlich könnte ich gewisse Optimierungen ganz unten mit dem Lötkolben vornehmen. Vielleicht käme ich ja nie wieder zurück, weil ich auch einen fatalen Kurzschluß hätte auslösen können, woraufhin die Maschine mit mir selbst als Benutzer zusammenbräche; aber wenn ich Glück hätte, könnte ich wirklich an der Maschine etwas ändern. Aber leider halte ich diesen Traum für absolut kontraindiziert angesichts der momentanen Industriestrategie, die, wie gesagt, darauf setzt, die Differenz zwischen Programmierern und Benutzern zu verewigen: Auf der einen Seite die Leute, die den Code kennen und schreiben können, auf der anderen Seite die Leute, die bloß seine Effekte als psychodelische Räusche wahrnehmen. Ich sähe diese Differenz gerne abgebaut, weil man allmählich unter diesem Computeranalphabetismus leidet. Aber letztlich gibt es, glaube ich, ein logisches Problem mit diesem Traum selber. Der Computer, müßte man wohl sagen, kann wie alle anderen Systeme nie reflexiv sein. Es würde die Rechenkapazität jedes denkbaren Computers übersteigen, seine eigene Hardware noch bis zum kleinsten Element für uns zu repräsentieren, er müßte sich mehr als verdoppeln, er müßte sozusagen unendlich sein, um eine Abbildung seiner eigenen endlichen Kapazitäten zu geben. Das kann er aber nicht, also bleibt immer ein blinder Fleck in der ganzen Maschinerie. Und dieser blinde Fleck läßt sich eigentlich nur durch Geschwindigkeitssteigerungen wegzaubern, aber nie beseitigen.

Weibel: Ich sehe die Zukunft so: In der modernen Kunst bedeutete die Abstraktion die Abschaffung der externen Referenz. Dann folgte die Abschaffung der internen Referenz, auf die Seele. Schließlich konnte die Maschine eben mit sich selbst sprechen.

Kittler: Ich glaube nicht, daß das kommt, daß die Autoreferenz eingeführt würde. Alle möglichen Fremdreferenzen werden eingeführt werden. Computer werden tun, als ob sie riechen, duften, singen und sonstwas. Sie werden nie so tun, als ob sie rechnen. Aber genau das würde ich wünschen: daß sie ihr eigenes Rechnen zugänglicher machen.

Friedrich A. Kittler Conversation between Peter Weibel and Friedrich A. Kittler

Weibel: How would you define the difference between a typewriter and a computer?
Kittler: Before settling on the differences it seems trivial but not quite unnecessary to say that there are in fact more similarities between the two than is commonly supposed. If what Andrew Hodges said about the unfortunate young Alan Turing is true, that the inventor of all computers had such miserable handwriting as a boy that he failed English public school, then the concept of the first universal discrete machine was the immediate result of the unsuccessful designs for a typewriter that Turing did at the age of fourteen. The anecdote illustrates how closely related they are. The wholesale standardization of script and letters really begins with the typewriter replacing handwriting, from 1870 onwards, not just in the printing industry which had remained quite a public affair, but in each individual job and at every desk, while the computer in a radical way only carries on the standardization of signs. It not only standardizes signs, but also analyzes their quantity until it turns out that under the auspices of the telegraph just two of them are sufficient. The minimum of twenty-six letters plus gap for a standard typewriter, in the days of Remington, initially without capitals, comes down to the pair '0' and '1'. However binarization opens up completely new possibilities for storage and processing. As long as you are confined to a random selection of so many

Greek or Latin letters, operations can only be carried out by structuring some chaotic territory beyond script itself, such as voice, for instance. Naturally, letters themselves cannot interact, they are what they are because they have historically evolved that way. In contrast, the two scriptural states represented by the physical correlation of the binary signs 0 and 1 can be fed back to each other, something quite unthinkable with conventional letters. How would you get a feedback effect of a and b? Whereas you may very well feedback 0 and 1 in sequence to each other. Hence all the differences result in the fact that typewriting and other scriptural systems have essentially remained mere storage systems, while, because the computer has also taken on the function of transmitting and processing data, it is able to further manipulate data. Superficially you could say it is a typewriter which not only types, but is also able to read itself.
Weibel: Could you say that the standardization into two denominations has brought about some universalization? With the typewriter you could only generate letters, whereas with the computer you can generate images as well. However, are image and text in fact not simply codes subservient to the binary code and only thus may I produce not just text, but also images by computer?
Kittler: This is a difficult question, particularly in view of the generation of sound that is possible in addition to the generation of images we find so fascinating today, and which is just as sophisticated, but has recently been overlooked. In the nineteenth century, the good old telegraph, for instance, could already produce music with its perforated strips if you ran them faster than you could read or write. We know it is the fact that the telegraph was producing various kinds of frequencies and noises which, in 1877, inspired Edison to invent the phonograph, the precursor of the gramophone. In this respect there is always the potential for treating such things in a way other than textually, by sheer misuse. The paradox with the generation of sounds and images by computer seems to be that it was necessary for

other media technologies to first produce the fundamental revolutions in the categories of sight and sound before it became possible for the computer as such to embrace the production of images. By revolution I also mean the conception of images for the very first time in history, following the example of letters, as subdivisions of finite quantities of elements, similar to Cantor's Dust. Ironically, Georg Cantor, with his mathematical spot quantities, was a contemporary of the Pointillist School of painting which subdivided paintings into specks of colour, and of the physicist Paul Nipkov, who as a student in Berlin, on Christmas day in 1884, developed the basic principle for television as a discrete linear reading of images. This is not what was done with film which indeed involved cutting between individual stills, which themselves were nevertheless still represented as a unified entity, recording and projecting real numbers. Only the revolution replacing real numbers and their infinite number of places behind the decimalpoint with calculable quantities of entire numbers has been able to bring about the modern manipulation of images. John von Neumann's observation that the measurement of real numbers and of analogue computers always contained some immanent noise error, whereas the error rate of calculating digitalized numbers can be indefinitely reduced seems to provide theoretical proof that something like ‹imaging› exists today. And CDs are the first historical effect of the fact that you can reproduce better signals by splitting, i. e. disfiguring signals, than by analogue fidelity which the gramophone had always been pursuing.

Weibel: Is the computer then the first step towards standardizing vision, just as the typewriter standardized writing?

Kittler: Indeed, images are only the first step. You can see the precursors for the realm of pixels in television preparing you for the computer, or even as early as the principle of ‹dithering›, invented in the 19th Century for graphic printing. Long before computers started to mix pixels because they did not have the colour facilities required for reproducing Photorealism, lay-out technicians in the 19th Century had developed the technique for newspaper reproduction: grey dots, randomly dispersed, which, when seen at a distance, made up a face. Of course this conception of a theory of vision contradicts any European tradition of vision since Plato.

Weibel: Would you say that the basic foundations for an alphabetization of the image were laid in the nineteenth century, from Pointillism to repro-techniques, in that the attempt was made to split the image into tiny individual spots similarly to splitting writing up into individual letters, and that the terrain for a mathematicalization of the image was prepared before 1900?

Kittler: Yes. The basic principles were laid down then, even though certain things like algorithms or digital image processing were not invented until ten years ago. And perhaps something else as well had to be added which has been around in theory since 1917, but was only brought into real prominence by Norbert Wiener, namely, using feedback as a means of reproducing images onto images or reapplying the mathematical representation of an image onto that image. Ever since, you can make up an image by calculation from another image, for instance by auto-correlating an image with itself or subjecting it to a Fourier Transformation. These seem to be the real advances, quite contradictory to conceive of an image no longer as given fact, but as an intermediate stage in a mathematical process.

Weibel: I also believe that the differentiation between subject and object is much less clearly defined with the computer than with the typewriter. If an image can describe itself or self-reproduce, can the picture turn into its own observer? And does this affect our own observation, how we perceive an image?

Kittler: Yes. No other machine has so far been able to reproduce all the human functions, they had all just represented partial aspects, if you are permitted at all to see it in such anthropological or anthropomorphic terms, which I hesitate to do. Only the computer is a self-regulating system, a ‹subject› in Kant's sense, equipped with all the ‹capabilities› of what we accept as human. In analyzing an image it demonstrates the capacity to differentiate, even in a reflexive manner. This is why we would disappear almost completely as subject. Programmes are getting increasingly capable of controlling themselves, and all the trends in computer application are moving toward replacing textual commands and commando logic with image-operated programmes. The awful Windows programmes for DOS, right to X-Windows for UNIX have led to a flood of images concealing what is, after all, still just a system of signs embedded in a circuit board. Thus the user is more or less reduced to a domesticated animal, because it is getting impossible to cut through the user-friendly graphic surface to gain access to the systems code below.

Weibel: What do you think about the theory that both the image and the observer are transformed simultaneously and affect each other? With the typewriter this was not the case. But with computer technology the image is transformed during the very act of observation. And there might be the possibility that the state of the observer could instantly be recorded electromagnetically, which in turn could immediately transform the image.

Kittler: Are you saying the observer controls the image?

Weibel: Perhaps, yes.

Kittler: Implementing this effect by arranging a kind of typewriting keyboard on the floor could perhaps be feasible, but I don't yet think it happens automatically in computer technology, unless perhaps with Virtual Reality which is sensitive to eye-movement.

Weibel: That's what I mean. What would this imply for your theory?

Kittler: I haven't yet experienced Virtual Reality, and I'm not particularly anxious to do so. What would this imply for my theory? Actually, my theory is not sufficiently realistic to be applied to all aspects of life.

Weibel: Alternatively, let's say for the interface. How, in your view, does it affect the theory of the interface?

Kittler: I would suspect that in sensing eye movement by opthalmokinesis (the foundation, by the way, of Husserl's theory of human perception), it would no longer be man who is the observer, instead he would be observed for the very first time. His observational act, his eye movement, would in turn be observed by sensors sitting right in front of the eye and instantaneously registering any movement back with the machine, whereupon it is possible for the machine to react immediately. Eyes and mouth, long accepted as the last refuge of intimacy, will be integrated in a feedback logic which is not ours, but that of the machine. The affect of VR would not be so unsettling if we did not realize that we are being observed by something that we cannot acknowledge as subject or persona in the traditional European sense, and which nonetheless constantly demonstrates that it sees us without revealing itself.
Weibel: Does that mean for you the machine's autonomy is getting out of control?
Kittler: Yes. As you know, I'm paranoid.
Weibel: How would this fit in with the infamous Project of Modernity, I mean the machine getting out of control, its autonomy?
Kittler: I have always read the famous ‹Project of Modernity› as a project to produce the ultimate missile. This is why we are going to Peeneemünde on 3 October 1992 to celebrate the 50th anniversary of the V 2 as mother of all missiles. In the words of Thomas Pynchon in his romanticized account of the V 2, the Project of Modernity had essentially been one of arms and media technology; all the better that it was shrouded in a pretty phraseology of democracy and the communication of consensus.
Weibel: How, then, do you explain the fierce ideological resistance to the machine during the Project of Modernity? In 1839 Henry Fox Talbot saw that the machine was now able to paint (‹it is the picture that makes itself›). He writes ‹Some Account of the Art of the Photogenic drawing, or, the Process by which Natural Objects May Be Made to Delineate themselves with-

out the Aid of the Artist's Pencil›. But in 1844 he gave the book the title ‹Pencil of Nature› instead of ‹Pencil of Machine›. He could not concede that the artist was being replaced by the machine. However, the independence of the machine was the prerequisite for the Project of Modernity; this was what set off the logic of autonomy, of the autonomy of form and colour etc. Yet, still the art scene is trying to keep the machine out. What kind of fears are we dealing with here, that people are unwilling to accept that the revolution of the machine, including missiles, has initiated the Project of Modernity?
Kittler: I would say it has to do with the history of our most sanctified institutions, where a lot of the necessary research is still outstanding. I should think the conflict erupted so violently in the eighteenth centuries between the new engineering faculties such as at the Paris Ecole Polytechnique, set up for military reasons to work on the factual achievement of modernization, and the traditional Universities whose long-established lobby was still able to dominate public opinion. It was extremely hard for the new practical sciences to enlist the kind of cultural acceptance their achievement deserved. In Germany, for instance, the much reviled Kaiser Wilhelm II who had a very favourable attitude towards technology had to use the full force of his authority to enable the Technical College at Charlottenburg to issue doctorates as of 1900. All the German Universities had protested fiercely against any kind of public acclaim of engineering. This kind of conflict is still being waged today by some people, for example in Frankfurt, who believe that language represents one aspect of civilization, and technology quite another. They utterly fail to see that anything we are now talking about, like speech and writing, language and typing, language and grammar, language and codification provides ample proof of the fact that language itself represents a kind of technology in the widest sense. It must be some ancient, out-of-date definition of language and civilization that is obstructing that view, especially in Europe. In Japan, where things were different, it has been much easier.

Weibel: I, too, believe this to be a central thesis, that technology is itself a language and language a technology. Can you elaborate on that?
Kittler: We may assume that there was some kind of primeval language, breathed by a transitory voice, ‹a Being which is disappearing while it is›, as Hegel would say: a pure voice getting lost as no gramophone can record it. But really, today no one believes in the existence of such a primeval language of the spontaneous, instead we assume that some kind of sign-system of scrawls, some graphic script must have been needed for speech to evolve, as language would have disappeared from the face of the earth without the help of some kind of memory-support system. If there are sign-systems, and as long as they exist to cut up and dissect that strange flow of speech, according to Homer emanating from its enclosure in the lips, rendering it memorizable as pictograms, alphabets or the like, then language is subjected to nothing else but the same sort of thing that happens to the multitude of optical phenomena when they are hacked into 24 recorded stills per second for film. As this is an obviously technical process with film, I cannot see why we shouldn't project this technological conception onto language. The introduction of the Greek vowel alphabet on which we are, after all, based has provided the clear demonstration that speech itself has been transformed by the introduction of script, the alphabet as virtuoso analysis of ‹natural› speech on which all typewriters are based. If, then, democracy, philosophy, literature, all the peculiarities first available to the Greeks had only been made possible by the introduction of script and do not occur in analphabetic civilizations, then language must be defined essentially by writing and if the codification of its signs changes, so do its structures.
Weibel: Does the binary code thus ultimately entail the final demise of script?
Kittler: It is rather more of a turning-point, and not the end. The problem today is how to convince ourselves, our listeners,

and consumers in general to apply themselves seriously to this new sign-system, instead of forever simply enjoying its side-effects. It is my concern, though, with Virtual Reality, that people will get immersed in all the gadgetry of the computer without bothering to learn the signatory system itself. Taking the trouble to learn how to programme will, unfortunately, be rewarded with the acquisition of power, and those few who are capable of writing programmes ...

Weibel: So, are we at the beginning of a new age of writing in the binary code?

Kittler: Yes. Or can you detect any other new codes or analogue technologies beyond the binary code? I am asking, because it is so difficult to see any way out, in spite of the many attempts to re-emerge from this most primitive of all codifications.

Weibel: What it amounts to is that script is now so all-powerful that it can generate images.

Kittler: Yes. Perhaps one should say, in the sense of what the late Willem Flusser meant, that script has only become so mighty because it has now become capable of generating images. Images have always been one aspect of writing, as in the case of the war between Jesuits and Protestants, or the Camera Obscura and Bible lecturers. But today's script is capable of generating images and sounds because the differentiation between letters and numbers has dissolved in the digital code. It has always been a peculiar story. We are pretty convinced that no European language has ever existed that did not somehow include numerical denominations, whether it be the Greek alphabet where the first letter alpha also denotes the number one, and beta likewise two, or be it the Romans with their funny lines representing a numerical system, right up to the middle ages when Arabic numbers began to be imported. Nonetheless, a differentiation between letters and numbers had always been prevalent: and the letters representing numbers in particular languages meant that the numbers were usually of international origin, and therefore unpronounceable. Now of course the signal can be read either as letter or as number, if not by man, then by the computer which we have already defined above as a self-reading typewriter. The inner workings of the hardware will read anything numerically or as a currency flow of signals, but a letter is easily represented numerically, whereas the reverse representation of numbers by letters – as was attempted in other eras – has definitely failed.

Weibel: But can it nevertheless be said that the vision of a universal language, from Lullus to Leibniz, has now come true?

Kittler: Indeed, and it was Leibniz who first made it available to us as a binary system of numbers.

Weibel: It means that letters are represented as digits and numerical systems. Such a numerical system is in turn capable of reproducing images?

Kittler: Of course perspective represented the first case of a geometrical system generating pictures (though they were not yet algebraic). I am assuming – though we'd have to delve more deeply into the subject, which is more likely your domain, anyway – that the great effectivity of numbers is a result of their unlimited manipulation. With letters we are confined to controlling whatever may be expressed by our voices, and we cannot do that without referring back to the semantics or syntax of how we actually talk, and what has been taught as language by our parents and grandparents. Whereas with numbers any mathematician or gangster could come along and claim that the digit 1 would henceforth represent the square root of -1; similarly you may decide on the integral sign or change the sign for dividing, as Leibniz did, you may evolve new combine systems from such intervals, omit certain indices as Einstein did in his Tensor Calculations, in fact you may freely exploit any alphabet. Thus Cantor introduced the Hebrew alphabet into mathematics. Now there is no foreseeable end to the development of similar hierarchies or new denominational systems. Perhaps this represents the primordial post-modern manifestation, if you will: all the significant systems of all the peoples of the entire world are

now available for redefinition, there are no longer any bounds to what might be defined as a symbol, i. e. as operator.
Weibel: Does this render obsolete Whorf's Hypothesis that particular languages would set up specific worlds? Only because the world of the binary code is the same for everyone and universally accessible.
Kittler: Perhaps there are small differences in acceptance, as they would say these days. The distinguished and sophisticated syntax of the French language as laid down by the Academie Française has struggled powerfully, not just recently, but as early as the days of Richelieu, against adapting to the logic of the computer. There are too many syntactic dependencies in the French language which prevent the computer, with what the linguists would define as its agglutinating principles – everything co-existing in equality – from accessing a grammar consisting mainly of exclusive rules. To that extent I believe there are national differences in the level of acceptance for this kind of universality.
Weibel: But such a metaphysics of language à la Heidegger, language as ‹Dwelling of Being› no longer works in this age of technological transformation of the world.
Kittler: You'll never get me to say anything against Heidegger.
Weibel: I see, but I have another question to put to you on the problem of codification. Letters making up a word can only make sense for someone living with the relevant language and knowing it well enough. Otherwise, if I spoke French and you didn't know the language, my words wouldn't have any meaning. Now, in the case of my installation we have one single gesture (stepping on a sensor) with different meanings in three different worlds. Thus I am always doing the same thing, taking the same element from the code, only I am using it to demonstrate three different kinds of activities, three different formats or world-modes. So far this has been impossible with language.
Kittler: I disagree, with script it was possible. The classic case

would be provided by the shift key transferring you from the realm of small letters into the realm of capitals. In addition there are various ways on the keyboard of your PC to change modes between entering text or a command. Simply by depressing Control or Alternate you devalue the relevant letter on the key into a command carrying out whatever the sign may be. You enter the command as if by speech, but it is an act of talking with a computer and not with a human being. In general I would say that such differentiations within language never really existed, if you define it on the basis of a fictitious orality. However, if the premise is the technological union of language and script, then you have to check on the shift possibilities at each historical stage. I am thinking of royal signatures and the like: for example, the Roman emperors were for a while the only persons permitted or even obliged to use red ink, in order for their writs to indicate a different level and initiate into action whatever they said. Similarly I see your shifting between various world modes as a very scriptural operation.
Weibel: You could say that a capability already latently present in the typewriter is enormously amplified by the computer. Not only may you gain access to different worlds, but you can also create them yourself. With the typewriter these shifting ‹world modes› only involved switching from small to capital letters etc. and the computer has enormously advanced on that, so that now you really can engage in the creation of several worlds. But as they cannot co-exist simultaneously in actual reality they have to become virtual worlds.
Kittler: Yes. Being able to shift between worlds is quite new. In my examples I have attempted to look for the roots of shifting as basic principle for meta language and objective language. The fact that this can now proliferate endlessly is only made possible by our computational capacities.
Weibel: Do you detect any danger for yourself in the proliferation of virtual worlds?
Kittler: There is a threat ... I also have quite precise ideas of what

virtual worlds should be doing for me. My original tool is the soldering-iron with which I first assembled my very own Intel chips, quite illegitimately so in the eyes of Intel, but it worked. What I would like from Virtual Reality is also quite illegitimate in the eyes of the industry. I consider it a threat that VR will be capable of simulating any kind of holiday paradise from the Maledives to Madagascar. But no one except me could think of implementing the inner workings of the computer itself as virtual reality at the disposal of the user. I can imagine it beautifully. I would enter the computer, and slowly descend from the level of civilized language down to the assembly boards and the level of object code, entering the hardware where I could use my virtual soldering-iron within the machine as it is representing itself to me virtually, in order finally to effect certain optimum adjustments deep down inside with the soldering-iron. Perhaps never to return, I might cause a fatal short circuit whereupon the machine plus myself as user would collapse; but if I were lucky I could actually fundamentally change something within the machine. Unfortunately this ideal seems to me absolutely counter to the current strategy of the industry which seeks to entrench forever the difference between user and programmer, on one side people knowing and being able to write down the code, on the other side people who merely perceive its effects as psychedelic states of intoxication. I would like to see this difference removed because we are beginning to suffer under this kind of computer illiteracy. Ultimately, I believe, there is a logical problem with the ideal itself. We can well assume that the computer will never become reflexive. This would exceed the computing power of any conceivable machine if it would have to represent its hardware for us, right down to the smallest detail. It would have to more than just double itself, it would, in fact, have to become indefinite in order to represent its own limited capacity. This blind spot could only be conjured away, never remedied, by an acceleration of speed.

Weibel: This is my vision of the future: in modern art abstrac-

tion meant the disappearance of external references. It was followed by the disappearance of internal, psychological references. Thus the machine was finally able to talk to itself.
Kittler: I do not think this will happen, the advent of self-reference. All sorts of external references will be introduced, computers will pretend to smell and produce scent, to sing and what have you. But they will never pretend to compute. But this is precisely what I would wish for: that they should make their own processes of calculation more accessible.

Translated from German by Jörg von Stein

Peter Weibel
Geboren 1945 in Odessa, lebt in Buffalo, N.Y., Wien und Frankfurt/M. Studien der Literatur, Medizin, Logik und Philosophie in Paris und Wien: Promotion über mathematische Logik. 1976-1981 Lektor für ‹Theorie der Form›; 1979/80 Gastprofessor für ‹Medienkunst›; seit 1981 Gastprofessor für Gestaltungslehre und Bildnerische Erziehung an der Hochschule für angewandte Kunst in Wien; 1981 Gastprofessor am College of Art and Design, Halifax, Canada; 1981 Lektor für ‹Wahrnehmungstheorie›; 1983 Professor für Fotografie an der Gesamthochschule Kassel; 1984 Professor für visuelle Mediengestaltung an der Hochschule für angewandte Kunst in Wien; seit 1985 Associate Professor for Video and Digital Arts, Center for Media Study, State University of New York at Buffalo; seit 1989 Direktor des Instituts für Neue Medien an der Städelschule in Frankfurt/M.
Einzelausstellungen: 1975 Galerie nächst St. Stephan, Wien; 1977 Galerie Stampa, Basel; Galerie nächst St. Stephan, Wien; 1978 Stichting de Appel, Amsterdam; Galerie Heike Curtze, Wien; 1980 Galerie Stampa, Basel; 1982 Kulturhaus Graz; Kunsthalle Wilhelmshaven; 1986 Museo d'Arte Contemporaneo, Madrid; 1988 Museum für Angewandte Kunst, Wien; 1989 Galerie Grita Insam, Wien; 1990 Galerie Walcheturm, Zürich; 1991 Scanned Objects, Galerie Grita Insam, Wien; 1992 Peter Weibel: Malerei zwischen Anarchie und Forschung, Neue Galerie der Stadt Graz.
Gruppenausstellungen: 1966 Destruction in Art Symposion DIAS, London; 1968 Kunst und Revolution, Universität Wien; Underground Explosion, München, Köln, Stuttgart; 1970 1. Internationales Underground Film Festival, London; 1971 Experimenta 4, Frankfurt; 1972 Musik Dia Licht Film Festival, München; 1973 Austrian Art I.C.A. London, Galerie Demarco, London; Audiovisuelle Botschaften, Trigon, Steirischer Herbst, Graz; 1974 Projekt '74, Kunsthalle, Köln; 1975 Video Art, Philadelphia Art Museum, Philadelphia; Identität, Trigon, Steirischer Herbst, Graz; 1977 Documenta 6, Kassel; Video, Association Musée d'Art Moderne, Genf; Film als Film – von 1910 bis heute, Kölnischer Kunstverein, Köln; 1978 38. Biennale Venedig (Filmsektion); 1980 Paris-Berlin, Centre Georges Pompidou, Paris; Videowochen, Folkwang Museum, Essen; 1983 Art Aktuell, Städt. Galerie im Lenbachhaus, München; 1984 Arte Austriaca, Museo d'Arte Moderna, Bologna; Recent Acquisitions, Museum of Modern Art, New York; 1. Festival Nacional de Video, Circulo de Bellas Artes, Madrid; Clio-Award, New York; 31ième Festival de Cannes ‹prix national›; New Narration, American Film Institute; National Video Festival, Los Angeles; Organisation des 1. Europäischen Musikvideo-Festivals in Wien; Der künstliche Wille ‹elektronische Medienoper›, Ars Electronica, Brucknerhaus, Linz; 1985 Zeit – die 4. Dimension, Museum Moderner Kunst, Wien; A. I.V.A.C., Locarno Video Festival; Alles und noch viel mehr,

Kunstmuseum und Kunsthalle, Bern; Brainworks, Municipal Art Gallery, Los Angeles; Die neue Dimension der Skulptur, Forum Stadtpark, Graz; 1986 Immagine Elettronica, Galleria d'Arte Moderna, Bologna; Berner Film Festival; 1ère Biennale de la Photographie d'Arte, Paris; Skulptur in Österreich, Galerie Grita Insam, Wien; New Forms in Art, State University of San Francisco; Künstlerphilosophen, Kunsthaus, Zürich; Ars Electronica, Brucknerhaus, Linz; 1987 Freie Klänge – offene Räume, Ars Electronica, Linz; Animal Art, Steirischer Herbst, Graz; 1988 Das gläserne U-Boot, N.Ö. Landesregierung Kulturabt., Tabakfabrik Krems/Stein; Stimmen aus dem Innenraum, Oper (mit S. Widl, V. Export, P. Jünger), Ars Electronica, Kunst der Szene, Linz; Freizone, Dorotheengasse, Wien; 1989 Wien Wien 1960-1990, Museum für Moderne Kunst, Bozen, Ivano, Valsugana; Permanente, Mailand; Fotografie, Wissenschaft und neue Technologien, Facetten der Interaktion, Kunstmuseum, Düsseldorf; Das Spiel des Unsagbaren, Secession, Wien; Das gequälte Quadrat, Schloß Buchberg, Gars/Kamp; Die Optik der Objekte, Kunstsalon im Kulturhaus, Graz; 1990 Art Cinéma, Vidéo, Ordinateur, Rencontres Internationales, Vidéothèque de Paris; Kunstmesse Frankfurt, Galerie Grita Insam, Frankfurt; Immagine Elettronica, Palazzo del Diamante, Ferrara; Le désenchantement du Monde, Villa Arson, Nizza; Parterres, Galerie Monika Detterer, Frankfurt; Galerie Schneider, Freiburg; Zeichen im Fluß, Museum des 20. Jhdts. Wien; 1990 Stadtmuseum Prag, Museum Moderner Kunst Zagreb; Im Licht des Monitors, Kunstverein Horn, Stadtmuseum Prag, Kunstverein Graz; Österreichische Skulptur, Secession, Wien; Raum annehmen III, Galerie Grita Insam, Wien; 1991 Where are you? Where am I? Arbeiten mit Polaroid, Galerie Grita Insam, Wien.
Bücher: Wiener Aktionismus und Film (mit V. Export), Kohlkunst Verlag, Frankfurt 1970; Studien zur Theorie der Automaten (mit F. Kaltenbeck), R&B, München 1974; Erweiterte Fotografie, Secession, Wien 1981; Mediendichtung, Protokolle 82/2, Jugend und Volk, Wien 1982; Im Bauch des Biestes, Logokultur, Hrsg. Hochschule f. angewandte Kunst, Wien 1987; Clip, Klapp, Bum. Von der visuellen Musik zum Musikvideo (hrsg. mit Veruschka Body), Dumont Taschenbuch 198, Köln 1987; Die Beschleunigung der Bilder. In der Chronokratie. Reihe ‹um 9›, Benteli Verlag, Bern 1987; Jenseits der Erde, Hora Verlag, Wien 1987; Kurt Gödel – ein mathematischer Mythos (80 Minuten). Ein Filmporträt mit Werner Schimanovich. ORF 1987; Inszenierte Kunstgeschichte. Katalog zur Ausstellung im Museum für angewandte Kunst. Hrsg. Museum für angewandte Kunst, Wien 1988; Im Netz der Systeme (hrsg. mit G. J. Lischka), Kunstforum 103/1989; Vom Verschwinden der Ferne. Telekommunikation und Kunst (hrsg. mit Edith Decker), Dumont 1990.

Susanne Craemer
Geboren 1958 in Trier, studierte nach ihrem Redaktionsvolontariat Allgemeine und Vergleichende Literaturwissenschaft, Italienisch und Theaterwissenschaft an der FU Berlin; sie promovierte 1992 über Bilder des Eigennamens in den Selbstbiographien Goethes, Stendhals und Kierkegards (Goethe als gotisches Münster); Lehraufträge (Ästhetik, Symboltheorie) an der FU Berlin; kunsthistorische Übersetzungen a. d. Ital. für Wagenbach Berlin' Buchbesprechungen, Ausstellungsrezensionen.

Hubert Damisch
Geboren 1928 in Paris. Lehrt Kunsttheorie und Kunstgeschichte an der École Pratique des Hautes Études und an der École Normale Supérieure in Paris. Freier Mitarbeiter für zahlreiche amerikanische und französische Kunstzeitschriften. Veröffentlichte mehrere Bücher und Aufsätze zur Kunstgeschichte.

Robert Fleck
Geboren 1957 in Wien. 1978 bis 1981 Mitarbeit in Österreichischen Galerien. Studium der Philosophie, Geschichte und Kunstgeschichte in Innsbruck und Paris, u. a. bei Deleuze und Foucault. Frankreich-Korrespondent von ART und Kurator im Auftrag des Österreichischen Bundesministers für Unterricht und Kunst für die Jahre 1992 und 1993. Veröffentlichte Bücher: ‹Avantgarde in Wien – Die Geschichte der Galerie Nächst St. Stephan 1954-1982›, Wien 1982; ‹Weltpunkt Wien – Un regard sur Vienne›, Wien und Paris 1985; ‹Gleichheit auf den Barrikaden – Die Revolution von 1848 in Europa›, Wien 1991; ‹Kann Österreich das Jahr 1994 überleben›, Wien 1991.

Friedrich A. Kittler
Geboren 1943 in Sachsen, Studium der Literaturwissenschaft und Philosophie in Freiburg/Br., bis 1986 Privatdozent in Freiburg, Gastprofessuren in Stanford, Berkeley, Santa Barbara und Basel, seit 1987 Professor für Neugermanistik an der Ruhr-Universität Bochum, Mitglied am DFG-Projekt Literatur und Medienanalyse in Kassel und beim Collège international de philosophie in Paris. Buchveröffentlichungen u. a.: ‹Urszenen› (zus. mit Horst Turk), Frankfurt 1977; ‹Grammophon Film Typewriter›, Berlin 1986; ‹Aufschreibesysteme 1800/1900›, München 1987; Alan Turing, ‹Intelligence Service› (hrsg. zus. mit Bernhard Dotzler), Berlin 1987; ‹Dichter – Mutter – Kind›, München 1991.

Avital Ronell
Geboren in Prag, lebte in Israel, New York, Berlin, Paris, heute in Kalifornien. Lehrtätigkeit an der Universität in Berkeley. Schrieb als erste Theoretikerin 1983 einen philosophischen Essay über AIDS. Veröffentlichungen über Krieg, feministische Philosophie, Walter Benjamin, Nietzsche. Buchveröffentlichungen: ‹Dictations: On Haunted Writing›; ‹The Telephone Book: Technology, Schizophrenia, Electric Speech›; ‹Crack Wars: Literature/Addiction/Mania›.

Otto E. Rössler

Geboren 1940 in Berlin, 1966 Doktor der Medizin an der Universität Tübingen, 1967 Postdoc, Max-Planck-Institut für Verhaltensphysiologie in Seewiesen, 1969 Gastdozent am Center for Theoretical Biology der Staatsuniversität von New York in Buffalo. Seit 1977 Professor am Institut für Physikalische und Theoretische Chemie der Universität Tübingen. 1981 Gastprofessor für Mathematik an der Guelph University in Kanada. 1983 Gastprofessor am Center for Nonlinear Studies der Universität von California in Los Alamos. Zahlreiche wissenschaftliche Veröffentlichungen über deduktive Biologie, chemische Automaten, chaotische Attraktoren, Hyperchaos und Endophysik. ‹Endophysik›, Berlin 1992.

Paul Virilio

Geboren 1932 in Paris. Theoretiker der ‹Geschwindigkeit›, Begründer einer neuen Wissenschaft ‹Dromologie›. Leiter der École spéciale de l'architecture in Paris, Redaktionsmitglied von ‹Traverses›, Mitarbeiter von ‹Libération›. Buchveröffentlichungen in deutscher Sprache: ‹Fahren, fahren, fahren . . .›, Berlin 1978; ‹Geschwindigkeit und Politik›, Berlin 1980; ‹Der reine Krieg›, Berlin 1984; ‹Krieg und Kino›, München 1986; ‹Ästhetik des Verschwindens›, Berlin 1986; ‹Das öffentliche Bild›, Bern 1987; ‹Der negative Horizont›, München 1989; ‹Die Sehmaschine›, Berlin 1989; ‹Rasender Stillstand›, München 1992.

Slavoj Žižek

Geboren 1949 in Ljubljana, Jugoslawien. Philosoph und Psychoanalytiker, Begründer der slowenischen Lacan-Schule, Herausgeber der deutschsprachigen Zeitschrift der Lacan-Schule ‹Wo es war›. Buchveröffentlichungen u. a.: ‹Tout ce que vous avez toujours voulu savoir sur Lacan, sans jamais oser le demander à Hitchcock› (Hrsg. und Hauptbeitrag), Paris 1988; ‹Le plus sublime des hystérique – Hegel passe›, Paris 1989; ‹The Sublime Object of Ideology›, London 1989; ‹Ils ne savent pas ce qu'ils font – le sinthome idéologique›, Paris 1990; ‹Looking Awry – An Introduction to Lacan Through Popular Culture›, Cambridge 1991; ‹Liebe Dein Symtom wie Dich selbst›, Berlin 1991.

Christian Möller
1959 geboren in Frankfurt am Main. 1981-1986 Architekturstudium in Frankfurt. 1986-1988 Stipendiat an der Akademie der Bildenden Künste in Wien, Meisterschule Gustav Peichl.
1988-1990 Mitarbeiter im Architekturbüro Behnisch und Partner in Stuttgart. Seit 1991 eigenes Büro in Frankfurt und Mitarbeiter am Städelschule-Institut für Neue Medien, Frankfurt. Seit 1992 Lehrauftrag für virtuelle Architektur an der Städelschule in Frankfurt.

Dieter Sellin
13.2.57 in Düsseldorf geboren. Seit 1983 Videoarbeiten, Dokumentar-Kunstbänder, Videoskulpturen. Seit 1988 Lehrbeauftragter für den Videobereich an der Kunstakademie Düsseldorf. Seit 1990 künstlerisch wissenschaftlicher Mitarbeiter am Städelschule-Institut für Neue Medien, Frankfurt.
1989 Ars Electronica: van Gogh TV.

Gideon May
1964 in Amsterdam geboren. 1984 Assistent für Modefotografie. Von 1985 bis 1986 Assistent für Special Effects. 1987 bis 1990 Kamera-Assistent. 1990 Koch in einem italienischen Restaurant. Seit 1988 Programmierer für Computergrafik.
Projekte mit Jeffrey Shaw:
1987 Torino, Video Narcissus; 1988 Maastricht, The Legible City; 1989 Nagoya (Japan), Boston, The Legible City; 1990 Linz, The Imaginary Museum of Revolutions; 1991 Frankfurt, The Virtual Musem.

Bob O'Kane
am 16.10.1966 in Indien geboren, legte an der State University of New York in Buffalo im Fachbereich Kunst ein Diplom für Medienforschung ab.
Seit kurzem ist er Meisterschüler an der State University of New York in Buffalo und unterrichtet am Städelschule-Institut für Neue Medien, Frankfurt.

Akke Wagenaar
Geboren 1958 in den Niederlanden; studierte Technik und audiovisuelle Kunst an der Gerrit Rietveld Akademie in Amsterdam, Photographie und Schriftstellerei an der Cooper Union Art School in New York und Logik an der Universität Amsterdam.
Seit 1990 arbeitet sie und seit 1991 lehrt sie am Städelschule-Institut für Neue Medien in Frankfurt/Main. Sie erhielt zwei Stipendien vom holländischen Fonds für bildende Kunst.

Constanze Ruhm
Geboren 1965 in Wien; Hochschule für Angewandte Kunst; Meisterklasse für Visuelle Mediengestaltung bei Peter Weibel; Städelschule-Institut für Neue Medien, Frankfurt; Fotografie, Video, Computeranimation, Interaktive Computerinstallation (‹Un Coup de Des›, nach einem Text von Stephane Mallarmee).

Ulli Schaaf
Geboren am 6. März 1960; Studien FH Köln: Architektur 1980-85; TH Warschau: Nachdiplomstudium ‹Konservierung von Architekturdenkmälern›. Schwerpunkt: Entwerfen im historischen Umfeld, 1988-89. Uni Torun: Studium der Denkmal- und Museumskunde. Schwerpunkt: Bauaufnahme, Bauforschung und Dokumentation.
derzeitige Tätigkeit:
wissenschaftlicher Angestellter am Deutschen Zentrum für Handwerk und Denkmalpflege.

Dank:
Bundesministerium für Unterricht und Kunst, Wien
Bundesminister Dr. Rudolf Scholten
Ministerialrat Mag. Josef Secky
Merlin Carpenter
Isabelle Graw
Daniela von Heyl
Fa. Kamps
Ursula Kohnen
Thomas Locher
Nils Norman
Yvonne Parent
Ulli Rieger
Vincent Tavenne
Eva Thole
Ute Wieckhorst
Lisa Zeiger

Dieses Buch enstand anläßlich der Ausstellung
«On Justifying the Hypothetical Nature of Art and the Non-Identicality within the Object World»
Peter Weibel
in der Galerie Tanja Grunert, Köln, 5. Juni bis 1. August 1992

Auflage: 2000

Herausgeber:
Robert Fleck

Redaktion:
Heike Kempken

Autoren:
Susanne Craemer, Hubert Damisch, Robert Fleck, Friedrich A. Kittler, Avital Ronell, Otto E. Rössler, Paul Virilio, Slavoj Žižek

Übersetzungen:
Jeanne Haunschild, Wilfried Pranter, Jörg von Stein, Antje Quast

Ausstellungsarchitektur:
Christian Möller, Ulli Schaaf

Technische Betreuung und Realisation:
Städelschule-Institut für Neue Medien, Frankfurt
Dieter Beck, Bob O'Kane, Gideon May, Constanze Ruhm, Dieter Sellin, Akke Wagenaar
Tanja Grunert und Michael Janssen, Köln

Auslieferung/Distribution:
Buchhandlung Walther König, Köln

Grafik Design/Konzept:
Christoph Radl

Gesamtherstellung:
Druckerei Heinrich Winterscheidt GmbH, Düsseldorf

ISBN 3-88-375-166-9